1

The *Real* Utopia: The Kingdom of God

This Book
Is Presented To:

_____

Name   *Date*

By

∴

_____

Name   *Date*

Formally: "The Prince of Peace"

Publisher:
Happy Note Publishing Co. and Rev. Charles J. Guerra
Presents:
A Five Star Quality Book

"The *Real* Utopia: The Kingdom of God"

Charles J. Guerra
Catherine R. Guerra

Contributors

Capt. Zachary J. Cogon (U.S. Army Ret.)
Middletown, New York – 10940
This book
Includes:

Comments on same-sex marriage
Is the Bible the Inspired Word of God?
The Parables and Miracles of Jesus

*****

"Come unto me all ye that labor and are heavy laden, and I will give you rest." Matt. 11:28

*****

This Book is dedicated to:
My loving wife Catherine R. Guerra
(I will always love you, Kaye).
And
James F. Guerra (Beloved Brother)
Colonel and Mrs. Roy M. Oldford, Salvation Army (Ret)
Mr. & Mrs. Joseph Guerra
James Guerra (Nephew)
Joseph Guerra, Jr. (Nephew)
John Z .Cogon, Grandson

Book Cover Designed By:
John Z. Cogon
© 2003
By Capt. Zachary Cogon (US Army Ret.)

Table of Contents

*****

Preface

This is a true story about Jesus, the Son of God, and why He so willingly gave His life to reconcile all of us to His Father in Heaven.

Reading this powerful account of the life of our Lord will tell all of you what you need to know about Him. This extraordinary book will answer all your questions about Jesus and His ministry, the resurrection; what followed, and His ascension into Heaven, and so much more. As you read this book you'll feel as if you're right beside Jesus as He teaches, and suffers on the cross for our sins.

Never in the history of the world has there been the need for such a book! No author could have prepared it so warm, so life-like, and informative as did Charles J. Guerra. *You can even use it as a responsible study guide*. We strongly recommend that everyone read this book."

The Bishops and Specialist Doctors of United Church of the Apostles.

*****

Introduction

The story of the life of Jesus Christ is the greatest story that was ever told. It is a story of love, humility, grace, salvation, and so much more. It is the story of the Person of Jesus Christ, the Son of God, who came to earth to offer hope to all mankind.

To those of us who believe in Him, because of our faith, we have the promise of life after death. It is a promise that is satisfying and warm and loving in that when our lives end on earth, we know, because of Christ, our souls live on in a new world; a new place, prepared by Him where there is no pain and sorrow; no evil and hatred, or burdens that make our lives here on earth, in many cases, unbearable, because of the suffering so many of us go through.

This wonderful story, as revealed to the world in the gospels, is welcomed and beautiful. The story of Jesus Christ, simply put, is the story of God's love for all humanity. Because of God's tremendous love for us, He sent His only Son, Jesus Christ, who would give His own life for the sins of the world. Jesus Christ came to earth to provide a means of reconciliation with God for all of us who truly believe in Him and repent of our sins.

Before Jesus Christ willingly gave His life on the cross on Calvary's Hill, He spent most of His short life preparing posterity for what would be required of all of us in order to receive God's gift of everlasting life, the precious gift He promised to those who would be faithful. And, though He healed the sick and raised the dead, His primary concern was that mankind should have forgiveness of sin, and live forever.

Jesus, while in the flesh on earth, healed many. He even

raised the dead, as in the case of Lazarus, Jairus' daughter, and others. These *acts of mercy and love* were only performed by Him to, also, prove and/or demonstrate His divinity. Once He had captured the attention of the multitudes, He concentrated on teaching and preparing others who would carry on with His work when His mission on earth had been accomplished.

Jesus made it known to the world just who He was and His purpose for living. He made known to the world, many times, as when He told Martha, the sister of Lazarus, "I am the resurrection and the life. He that believeth in me though he was dead, yet shall he live" St. John: 11.

In essence, Jesus came to win the victory over death, and that by His resurrection, all might be raised up and live again if we believe in Him and have faith.

This wonderful, powerful, and great story teaches love, humility, and sacrifice as the attributes we must demonstrate if we are to live again forever, as God had originally planned. Unless we are able to live a life of humility, sacrifice, and love for our neighbors, Christ teaches, we cannot, and will not be heirs of God's great and wonderful gift of life everlasting. We must love our neighbors as we love ourselves... as we love God with all our heart and soul. In living this way, we acknowledge our belief in Christ/God and accept His teachings as outlined in the gospels.

Jesus said, "I am the way, the truth, and the life. No one cometh unto the Father but by me." St. John 14:6

In this story of the life of Jesus Christ, I have taken license, to elaborate only where there are instances not recorded, either in the gospels, or in other non-canonical writings or literature by historians and writers of Jewish antiquity. However, the story of Christ as I have written is factual and, in the few instances where it is not, is logical, in that the events and acquaintances *would* be possible and *could* have happened.

In many instances, I have sought to make the dialogue easier for all to understand in that I have rewritten some dialogue, etc. *In no way have I attempted to change the meaning of what Christ taught or to alter any sequence of events.*

As in the case of Thomas, Jesus' childhood friend; it is reasonable to assume that Jesus had many childhood friends and, without a doubt, spent more time with one than another. And, though we don't know much about His early years, I have taken the liberty to assume that Jesus had friends as do other children.

The wonderful thing about Jesus was that He, though He is God, became as any other person. This had to be the case. His sacrifice on the cross would have been meaningless had He not suffered and died as would any other man. However, it was His resurrection and victory over death that assures us that we, also, can live again. Without the resurrection, His life here on earth would have been in vain.

Enjoy the book. I know you will be truly blessed as you come to know exactly who Jesus is, His mission, and who murdered Him.

*****

The *Real* Utopia:
Chapter I

The Nativity

When we talk about the nativity, we are talking about the events concerning the birth of Jesus. The accounts of the Nativity of Jesus appear only in the Gospels of St. Matthew and St. Luke. Both of these gospels describe Jesus as being born in Bethlehem, in Judea, to the virgin, Mary.

Luke features what we choose to call the "Christmas" story in which Mary and her husband, Joseph, because of a census, travel to Bethlehem where Jesus is born and placed in a manger. A manger is a "feed trough" found in a stable. In biblical times they were made from clay, mixed with stones or straw, or both, in which was placed feed for the animals to come and eat from.

In the Gospel of St. Matthew we read of wise men following a star to bring gifts to Jesus who is born in Bethlehem. We read, also, that King Herod orders the execution of all toddler boys born in Bethlehem at the time in order to make sure that Jesus, the "King of the Jews" is killed. However, an angel appears to Joseph, in a dream, and tells Joseph to take the child Jesus, and Mary, and flee to Egypt where they remain until after the death of King Herod. When they learn of King Herod's death, they return to Nazareth.

In describing the Nativity of Jesus I prefer to follow the Gospel of St. Luke, mostly, because his account includes several events prior to the birth of Jesus that do not appear in the Gospel of St. Matthew, e.g. the trip from Nazareth to Bethlehem, while only the Gospel of St. Matthew describes the flight to Egypt after the birth of Jesus.

The book of St. Luke begins with the mention of a certain priest named Zachariah whose wife was called

Elisabeth. The events herein took place in Judea when King Herod was ruler. Zachariah and Elisabeth, we are told, were righteous people and were obedient to all the commandments and ordinances of the Lord. They were old and had no children because Elisabeth was "barren."

As was the custom of his office as priest, it was Zachariah's responsibility, having been chosen by lot, to burn incense when he went into the "holy place" in the temple of the Lord. The "holy place" is that part of the temple which is the inner sanctuary where the Torah is kept and where incense is burned. Whatever was going on in the "holy place" was not visible to those in the temple.

And there appeared unto Zachariah an angel of the Lord standing on the right side of the altar of incense. When Zachariah saw him he was afraid. "Fear not, Zachariah," the angel said. "Your prayers have been heard. Your wife Elisabeth shall bear you a son and you shall call his name John. And many shall rejoice because of his birth."

Zachariah, of course, had to be completely in awe. For years, he and his wife had been trying to have a child. Now, out of nowhere, an angel comes before him and tells him his prayers were heard. Who knows what could have been going through his mind when he heard what the angel told him. He might have thought the devil was playing a trick on him. He listened as the angel continued, "He will be a joy and a delight to you who will be great in the eyes of the Lord and he will drink no wine or strong drink. He shall be filled with the Holy Ghost even from his mother's womb."

The humble priest continued to listen while those praying in the temple, outside of the sanctuary, had no idea of what was going on in the "holy place."

"And many of the children of Israel shall he turn to the

Lord their God," the angel said. He continued, "And he (John) shall go before Him in the spirit and power of Elias (the prophet), to turn the hearts of the fathers to the children, and the disobedient to the wisdom of the just; to make ready a people prepared for the Lord (the Messiah)."

Zachariah, than, asked the angel, "When will I know this of which you speak? For I am an old man and my wife is stricken in years." By his remark, Zachariah was telling the angel that what he was telling him was impossible because he and his wife were just too old. Zachariah, in order words, could not believe that what the angel was telling him was true. In his mind, he must have been thinking, "impossible!"

Then the angel of the Lord said, "I am Gabriel that stands in the presence of God; and I am sent to speak to you, and to show you these glad tidings. Until the day that these things shall come to pass, you shall be dumb and unable to speak because you didn't believe what I told you."

While all this was going on, the people in the temple were wondering what was happening in the inner sanctuary. "What could Zachariah be doing that he would tarry for so long?" And when the priest came out, the people perceived that he had seen a vision because he could not speak to them. And, he remained speechless. And after those days his wife Elisabeth conceived, and hid herself five months.

In the sixth month the angel Gabriel was sent by God to a city in Galilee called Nazareth to a virgin named Mary, espoused to a man called Joseph of the house of David. The angel spoke to her, saying, "Hail, you are highly favored. The Lord is with you. Blessed are you among women."

And when Mary saw the angel she was afraid, and

troubled, because of what he was saying and wondered why the angel spoke to her the way he did. The angel recognizing her fear replied, "Don't be afraid, Mary, for you have found favor with God. You will conceive and give birth to a son and call his name Jesus. He will be great and shall be called the Son of the Highest, and the Lord God shall give to Him the throne of His father David." The angel paused as Mary, on her knees, stared, almost hypnotized by the sight of Gabriel, and the words he spoke. The angel added, "And of His kingdom there shall be no end."

Then said Mary unto the angel, "How can this be: seeing I know not a man?"

And the angel answered and said unto her, "The Holy Ghost shall come upon you, and the power of the Highest shall overshadow you: therefore the holy child that shall be born of you shall be called the Son of God."

Mary, at the time the angel visited her, was about 12 or 13 years of age. At the time, she was already engaged to be married to Joseph. Jewish girls in those days usually became engaged at an early age which was the first stage of a marriage, although the girl would normally remain with her parents for about a year before going to live with her husband and consummating her marriage. If the girl became pregnant before that time, she was disgraced. She could have even been stoned to death as an adulterous.

I make mention of Mary's age and wonder if you can even begin to imagine what could have been going on in Mary's mind when told she would conceive and give birth to a baby boy. How could she explain to Joseph? What would the rabbi and her neighbors conclude? Would they ever believe that God sent the angel Gabriel to her to inform her that she would give birth to the Son of God?

Those of you who have daughters and are always so

worried about the trials and problems you have raising them cannot even begin to imagine, by today's standards of moral behavior, why the parents of young girls in Jesus' day could even consider allowing their daughters to be engaged at such an early age. But that was their custom in those days as it was in the early days of the U.S. when men married young girls to bear children, hopefully boys, who would be born to work with their fathers doing farm work, pitching hay, raising stock, and farming the land.

*****

While so much was going on in Mary's mind, the angel told Mary, "Your cousin, Elisabeth, has also conceived a child in her old age and this is the sixth month with her who was also called barren. With God nothing is impossible!"

Then, without hesitation, Mary exclaimed, "Behold the handmaid of the Lord! Let it be unto me according to your word." And the angel Gabriel left her.

Mary, then, gathered together some of her clothes and took some food and, without telling anyone, left Nazareth and went to visit Elisabeth. And when she entered into the house of Zachariah and Elisabeth saw her, the baby she was carrying leaped for joy and she was immediately filled with the Holy Ghost. (Verse 41)

With a loud voice, Elisabeth said, "Blessed are you among women, and blessed is the fruit of your womb." Mary stood with her for about four months and left to return to her own home.

*****

Soon thereafter Elisabeth gave birth to a son. Her neighbors and relatives shared great joy with her for they knew the child was from God. On the eighth day the child was circumcised and they called him Zachariah, after his father. But Elisabeth objected and said, "Not so! His name shall be called John!"

When Elisabeth said this, the people turned to Zachariah and wanted to know how he felt about calling the child John.

"Should he be called Zachariah after you, the father? Or should he be called John?"

Zachariah, who was still unable to speak at the time called for a writing tablet and wrote, "His name shall be called John!" No sooner had Zachariah revealed what he had written and his mouth was "loosed" and he began praising God. (More is said of John who was born of Elisabeth who would prepare the way for Jesus Christ).

Mary returned to Nazareth and told Joseph where she had been and, also, about how the angel of the Lord, Gabriel, visited her and gave her the news of her being favored by God. She explained to Joseph that she was told by the angel that she would give birth to a child whose name she should call Jesus who was to be the Son of God.

This had to come as a shock to Joseph who was a very religious man. He just couldn't believe what Mary was telling him. But, while he thought on what Mary had told him, the angel of the Lord appeared to him in a dream, saying, "Joseph, son of David, don't be afraid to take Mary to be your wife. The child she has conceived is of the Holy Ghost. She shall give birth to a son and you shall call his name Jesus for he shall save his people from their sins." After Joseph awoke from his sleep, he did as the angel instructed and took Mary to be his wife.

*****

And it came to pass in those days, that there went out a decree from Caesar Augustus that all- the world should be taxed. It was necessary, then, that the people are counted. So, Joseph and Mary, being great with child, went from Galilee, from Nazareth, unto Judea, to the City of David which is called Bethlehem. Joseph had to report to Bethlehem because he was of the house and lineage of David. There, he and his wife would be counted for tax purposes. And so it was that while the holy couple were in Bethlehem the time had come for Mary to give birth.

Because of the great multitude of those who had come to Bethlehem to be counted, Joseph and Mary were unable to find a room in any of the inns. Because of the sympathy and kindness of the wife of a man who owned one of the inns had for the holy couple, they were given permission to stay in a stable owned by the owner of the inn.

St. Luke, Chapter 2 verse 7 tells us, "And she brought forth her firstborn son and wrapped him in swaddling clothes and laid him in a manger because there was no room for them in the inn."

In the darkness of the night, nearby, there were shepherds keeping watch over their flocks. And, an angel called out to them, saying, "Fear not: for, behold, I bring you good tidings of great joy, which shall be to all people. For unto you is born this day in the city of David a Savior which is Christ the Lord. You shall find the babe wrapped in swaddling clothes, lying in a manger." Suddenly, than, the sky shone bright and a great multitude of angels and heavenly hosts appeared and began joyfully praising God saying, "Glory to God in the highest, and on earth, peace, good will toward men!"

After the angels departed, leaving the shepherds to wonder because of what they had just experienced, one of them suggested, "Let us now go even unto Bethlehem, and see this thing which is come to pass, which the Lord hath made known unto us."

After they had looked for a while they found Joseph, and Mary, and the babe lying in a manger. And when they had seen it, they made known abroad the saying which was told them, by the angel, concerning this child. And all they that heard it wondered at those things which were told them by the shepherds.

*****

Now when Jesus was born in Bethlehem of Judaea in the days of Herod the king, behold, there came wise men from the east to Jerusalem saying, "Where is he that is born king of the Jews? We have seen his star in the east and have come to worship him." (From the Gospel of St. Matthew, Chapter 2).

When Herod the king had heard these things, he was troubled, and all Jerusalem with him. The king called for all his chief priests and scribes and assembled them in one place demanding where Christ would be born.

They replied, "In Bethlehem, of Judea: for it was written by the prophet, 'and thou Bethlehem, in the land of Juda, art not the least among the princes of Juda: for out of thee shall come a governor, that shall rule my people Israel.'"

And then King Herod summoned unto him the Wise Men and inquired of them what time the star appeared. King Herod told them, "Go to Bethlehem and search diligently for the young child. When you have found him, bring me word again, that I may, also, come and worship him."

After they had heard King Herod speak, the three Wise Men considered the kings motives and plainly concluded that the King's plan was to kill the new-born child. The three Wise Men were able to see the madness and envy in the king's eyes. For certain, King Herod was not going to share his throne with anyone; let alone a child. According to his chief priests and advisors, the birth of Jesus, the Messiah, had been foretold by the prophets. The king would do anything to make sure the child was destroyed.

The king was hoping that the three Wise men believed him and would get back to him informing him where the child was. He even had the three Wise men followed after they departed, but they were able to elude those that followed, further frustrating King Herod.

(Concerning the three wise Men mentioned in the Gospel of St. Matthew):

The Gospel of St. Matthew is the only Gospel to mention the three wise Men. The question now is, who were they? The three Wise Men were known as "Magi". They were astrologers, or Kings from the east.

The term, Magi, refers to the priestly <u>caste</u> of <u>Zoroastrianism</u>. As part of their religion, these priests paid particular attention to the stars, and gained an international reputation for <u>astrology</u>, which was at that time highly regarded as a science. Their religious practices and use of astrology caused derivatives of the term *Magi* to be applied to the <u>occult</u> in general and led to the English term *magic*. Translated in the <u>King James Version</u> as *Wise Men*, the same translation is applied to the wise men led by <u>Daniel</u> of earlier Hebrew Scriptures (<u>Daniel 2:48</u>). The same word is given as *<u>sorcerer</u>* and *<u>sorcery</u>* when describing "<u>Elymas</u> the sorcerer" in <u>Acts 13:6–11</u>, and <u>Simon Magus</u>, considered a <u>heretic</u> by the early Church, in <u>Acts 8:9–13</u>.

★★★★★

Chapter II

Joseph Takes Mary and Jesus to Egypt
Their Return to Nazareth

The three Wise Men saw a star and followed it rejoicing with exceeding great joy (St. Matthew 2:10). They followed the star which led them to the stable where Christ was born. And when they entered, they saw the child with Mary, His mother, and fell down and worshipped the child. They, also, brought gifts for the child. They presented Him with gold, frankincense, and myrrh.

After the three Wise Men had worshipped the new born baby and presented Him with gifts, they quickly departed because they were warned, in a dream, by God that they should not return to King Herod.

When the three Wise Men left, the angel of the Lord appeared to Joseph in a dream, saying, "Arise and take the young child and His mother, and flee into Egypt, and remain there until I bring you word: for Herod will seek the young child to destroy Him." So, Joseph rose up and took his wife and Jesus and left for Egypt.

King Herod, when he saw that he was mocked by the three Wise Men became fanatically belligerent. He soon sent forth his soldiers and slew all the children that were in Bethlehem, and in all the coasts thereof, from two years old and under, according to the time which he had diligently inquired of the Wise Men.

Then was fulfilled that which was spoken by Jeremiah the prophet, saying, "In Rama was there a voice heard, lamentation, and weeping, and great mourning, Rachel weeping for her children, and would not be comforted, because they are not."

The Bible states that there were three Wise Men,

Gaspar, Melchior, and Balthasar. The Bible doesn't tell us if there were more than three though there could have been, but we've no way of knowing. It is a common misconception that the Wise Men visited Jesus at the stable on the night of His birth. In fact, the Wise Men came days, months, or possibly even years later. That is why Matthew 2:11 says the Wise Men visited and worshiped Jesus in a house, not at the stable.

We know that these men were from the east; more than likely from Persia, modern day Iran. These Wise Men more than likely knew of the writings of the Prophet Daniel who had become the chief of the court seers in Persia and prophesied concerning the coming birth of the Messiah (See Daniel 9: 24-27). The Wise Men were guided by a star known as the "Star of Bethlehem" which they referred to as "His Star" as indicated in Matthew 2:2.

*****

When Herod was dead, behold, an angel of the Lord appeared in a dream to Joseph in Egypt, Saying, "Arise, and take the young child and His mother, and go into the land of Israel: for they are dead which sought the young child's life." And he arose, and took the young child and His mother, and came into the land of Israel.

*****

After Joseph brought Mary and Jesus back from Egypt, they took up residence in Nazareth where Joseph worked at his trade as a carpenter. This pious and humble man also worked using metal and stone, producing practical objects for agricultural and domestic use.

During that time, Nazareth would have had a population of not more than 400 people so it was certain that Joseph found it difficult to earn enough for his family to survive. So, he often had to pack up his tools and go to neighboring towns to find work.

There were three social levels in Nazareth when Jesus grew up there. There were the rich who were usually the landowners and/or entrepreneurs; the poor who worked on the land, or at a variety of trades; finally, there were those who had neither land nor job and survived by begging. Joseph and his family belonged to the middle level.

Mary was physically robust and strong minded and, like Joseph, was respectful of the Jewish religious traditions. She and Joseph would have spoken the Aramaic Language and both would have known the Jewish Scriptures. It was Mary's job to teach Jesus Jewish Scripture and the stories therein. In those days, the scriptural stories were not only for religious education, they were also taught for entertainment purposes.

So, while Joseph struggled to provide for his family, it was Mary whose responsibility it was to instruct Jesus in the Scriptures; and the men, then, taught Jesus the Torah.

But, Jesus, as a child had time to play with the other children in the small town of Nazareth. He had lots of friends and they often played games imitating other people, especially the old.

When Jesus was a child, the most popular thing the children enjoyed doing was dancing. The children also played at holding weddings and imitating their rabbi mimicking religious ceremonies.

Jesus as a child had lots of friends in Nazareth. He had one friend in particular He spent a great deal of time with. His name was Thomas bar Abas. In the Aramaic Language, the word "bar" meant "son of". Abas, the father of Thomas, owned a great deal of land and often had Joseph work for him making a plow or other farming implements he needed to work his land. Because of this, Abas was often in Joseph's home consulting with him in the production of the objects Joseph was to make. Thomas was almost always with his father when he went to visit Joseph. So, Jesus and Thomas, being the same age, became close friends.

Both Jesus and Thomas had to spend hours each day being instructed in Jewish Scripture and, later, the Torah. But, when they had free time, Thomas would hurry up the street to see Jesus and they would play, or sit under a tree in Thomas' olive grove, talking about the Scriptures or other things of interest.

Jesus was exceptionally bright when it came to knowing the Scriptures and Thomas marveled at how Jesus could quote and recite Jewish Scripture, word for word. Thomas was interested in the Jewish Laws only to the extent of what he was required to know as a Jew. Jesus could never get enough knowledge. He even seemed to know things about Jewish Law and Scripture both He and Thomas hadn't even been taught.

Sitting in the shade under an acacia tree Thomas asked Jesus, "How is it you know so much more than I and the others about Scripture?"

"I know more than you and the others because maybe I study harder than you do, Thomas," Jesus answered.

"But, you're always talking about the Law as though they were part of you." Thomas sighed and added, with a smile, "Haven't you noticed the way Adina looks at you, Jesus? I think she likes you."

Jesus looked into Thomas's eyes and said, "I like her, too, Thomas. All the girls in Nazareth are nice."

"But isn't there one girl you like more than the others?" Thomas asked.

Jesus stood and answered, "I think we'd better be going home, now. Remember, Thomas, in four days it will be the

23

feast of the Passover and we are leaving with the caravan in the morning for Jerusalem. We must get home and help to prepare for the trip."

Thomas stood and said, "I forgot, Jesus. But, you're right. If I don't help my father, I'm sure to get a paddling."

Jesus smiled when Thomas said this. Jesus now was 12 years of age and soon would be ready to be bar mitzvah. The term bar mitzvah means "son of the commandments." All Jewish boys were automatically given this designation when they reached age 13. It signified the coming of age of the child. It is at this age that the boy becomes obligated to observe the commandments. A girl, on the other hand, is mitzvah at the age of 12 and she is referred to as "bat mitzvah" or "daughter of the commandments."

Jesus said goodbye to Thomas and went directly to His home. When he entered, His mother said, "Jesus! It's getting late! Were you with your friend, Thomas, this afternoon?"

"Yes, mother!" Jesus answered as He sat at a small table in the center of the room.

Mary turned to look at Jesus and said, "You must eat. Tomorrow we will join the caravan early so there will be no time for food in the morning."

Mary always set a plate for Jesus because she knew how hungry He would be after studying the Scriptures and, when He had the time, playing with the children in town. This day, Jesus was to eat matzos, some olives, garlic, grapes, and milk.

Jesus was all excited about going to Jerusalem to celebrate the Passover. He had been looking forward to it for a long time. He quickly pushed some olives into his mouth, swallowed some milk and, after picking up a piece of matzo, stood and turned to ask His father, "How far is it to Jerusalem, father?"

Joseph who was stuffing some things into a traveling sack turned to face Jesus and answered, "About 65 or 70 miles."

Jesus, then, took a bite of matzo bread and said, "I can't wait to see the Temple! Are you going to make a sacrifice?"

"We must!" Joseph said. "We are obligated to. We give thanks to God because of all His blessings."

"You've asked enough questions, Jesus!" Mary said. "Finish your food and go to sleep. Your father and I will wake you early. We must leave here at dawn or we will miss the caravan."

Jesus quickly ate His food and, after kissing Mary goodnight and hugging his father, He lay down and was soon sound asleep.

When Joseph woke Jesus it was still dark. He shook Jesus, saying, "Wake up, son. We must hurry."

Jesus quickly dressed and hurried to the door of their small home. When He stood outside He could see most adults He knew in the street; their donkeys pulling small carts containing their belongings and food for the long trip to Jerusalem.

Joseph wasted no time loading and attaching their donkey to the cart. After he was sure everything was secure and that they hadn't forgotten anything, he raised Mary up and sat her upon the donkey.

Then, he took hold of the rope he had around the animal's neck, pulled it gently and said, "Time to go." And, they, as did the others of Nazareth, hurried on their way to join up with the caravan that was headed for Jerusalem. Most Jewish travelers preferred joining a caravan when making a journey because they were safe from thieves who would rob them when, and if, they traveled alone.

*****

When they were a part of the caravan, Jesus heard, "Jesus! Jesus!"

Jesus turned to look and saw that it was His friend, Thomas, waving his arm so that his friend knew where he was.

They spent the first night with their friends and enjoyed the food they brought with them as they relaxed and talked about the Scriptures and the good time they were going to have in Jerusalem. While the adults relaxed, the children, including Jesus and Thomas, played games and danced until they were finally told to go to sleep.

The following day was hot and dusty. It was a difficult journey for lots of the older Jews. But, the younger men and women, and the children, always had a wonderful time with their dancing and storytelling when their long days' trek was over after they set up their camp for the evening.

As they sat near the fire, Joseph said, "We'll be in Jerusalem the day after tomorrow, Jesus. How do you feel?"

Jesus wanted the time to go by quickly. He couldn't get to Jerusalem fast enough. With all the walking and staying up late at night, He was, nevertheless, robust and full of energy. "I'm only sorry we live so far away, father."

Joseph looked at the night sky and sighed deeply. Then he looked at his son sitting and staring as if oblivious to all the activity going on.

Joseph, a small and timid man that he was, stood and walked to his little cart and removed a bucket. He put some water in it and held it so his donkey could drink. As the donkey drank some water Joseph said, "We're not so far from Jerusalem, son. Many of these people live much further away than we do." He smiled as he said, "Don't be so impatient. Before you know it we'll be in Jerusalem and we'll have a wonderful time." He placed the empty bucket back in the small cart, rubbed his two hands together and added, "Get some sleep, Jesus. It's getting late and we still have a long walk ahead of us."

Mary was already asleep close to the fire and Joseph lay down beside her and closed his eyes. Jesus watched as Joseph pulled a blanket over his stubby white beard and nestled close to His mother.

Jesus sat quietly listening to the noise of the camp. The animals were making their usual sounds and there were still some who were talking as some of the children were still playing and dancing. The young lad loved crowds of people and He would always be surrounded by huge crowds. He didn't know why He felt that way. He just knew that He did.

Jesus, as mentioned before, studied the Scriptures and it was noticeably apparent that He loved God very much. Even at such a young age He was able to recite Scripture by heart. He, especially, enjoyed the Psalms and had committed many of them to memory. As He sat looking about, He thought of how He could please God. He wanted to pray; and so He did.

Sitting alone, He said, "Make a joyful noise unto the Lord all ye lands. Serve the Lord with gladness; come before His presence with singing. Know ye the Lord He is God. It is He that hath made us and not we ourselves. We are His people and the sheep of His pastures. Enter into His gates with thanksgiving and into His courts with praise. Be thankful unto Him and bless His name. For the Lord is good, His mercy is everlasting and His truth endureth through all generations." Psalm 100

For whatever reason; Jesus wanted everyone about Him

to feel as He did about God. He, somehow, felt very close to God and sensed the importance for everyone to know as much as possible about Jehovah. He thought about what the Psalm He had just recited meant. He knew in His heart that whatever anyone had; their donkey, their little home, the food they ate; the clothes they wore, and their neighbors; everyone should praise God and thank Him every day; for the Lord is good and merciful. Someday, Jesus began to think; maybe He could make them understand these things more clearly.

The young lad, then, yawned and stood. He took a deep breath and then went to lie down on a blanket beside their cart.

*****

When morning came, Thomas and his father and mother joined Joseph, Mary, and Jesus and they continued their journey to Jerusalem. Pretty soon they would be able to see the Temple from a distance.

Jesus and Thomas, anxious as they were, hurried ahead of the caravan. Jesus became more excited as the miles went by. Thomas found it difficult keeping up with Jesus. Near the end of the day, just as the sun was beginning to set, Thomas caught up to Jesus. He was sitting atop a hill staring down at the holy city of Jerusalem.

Puffing and panting, out of breath, Thomas sat beside his friend and, being so exhausted, lay down on his back beside Jesus. Jesus looked at Thomas and said, "Look, Thomas! Jerusalem!" He pointed and Thomas forced himself to sit up.

To both these young boys, Jerusalem might have looked like one of the wonders of the world. The city was huge compared to their home town of Nazareth. It was still a few miles in the distance but they could sense the activity and movement that was going on.

Jesus stood and turned to help Thomas to his feet. They stared hard at the magnificent city and Jesus was excited and nervous as He stood and looked at the city where He would ultimately give His life for the sins of the world.

Jesus and Thomas remained atop the hill overlooking Jerusalem waiting for their families to arrive. Because it was late, they camped that night so they could be rested when they entered the holy city the following day.

That final night before entering Jerusalem had to be like torture for Jesus as He was noticeably excited and nervous. He turned in earlier than most of the others so that the morning would come faster.

The following morning, Joseph and Mary awoke earlier than usual. There were thousands of people who were with the caravan who were up earlier than they and who were already making their way to one of the huge gates entering the city.

When Joseph had awakened Jesus, their small cart was already loaded and ready to go. As Joseph gently poked at his son, he said, "Jesus! Wake up! Wake up!"

Jesus quickly opened His eyes and looked at His father. Then He looked about as He sat up. He could see that the people were already on the move heading towards the city. Jesus jumped to His feet and rubbed His eyes.

"Come along, Jesus," Joseph said as he pulled on the rope that was around his donkey's neck. Without saying another word, Mary, walking along side of Joseph, with Jesus following, left their camp site.

As they moved over the top of the mountain and down the western slope, they were able to see the holy city just below. The view was stunning. The sight was awesome. They passed an immense graveyard and then noticed the ground fell off sharply and was dotted with stands of pine and silvery green olive trees. From there, they followed others and went down into the Kedron Valley.

On the other side of the valley was a great tan wall. Then they were able to see a grandiose platform which was used as a place of worship. From there, Joseph, Mary, and Jesus passed through what was known as the "Beautiful Gate" and entered Jerusalem.

Once inside the walls of the great city, Joseph made his way to a small clearing and said, "Let us rest here for a while. We'll wait for Thomas and his father. They should be along soon."

Joseph removed a small stool from the cart and placed it on the ground near the cart. "Mary," he said. "Sit down and rest." Then, from the wooden cask, in the cart, Joseph used a ladle he had brought to scoop some water. "Here, Mary," he said. "Drink… you'll feel better."

Mary drank from the ladle as Joseph held it tightly. "Thank you," she uttered. Then, gently nudging the ladle, Mary said, "Give some to Jesus. He, too, must be thirsty."

When Joseph looked around, he saw that Jesus was gone. "He is not here," he said. Noticeably angry, Joseph sounded, "Now, where is that boy?" He turned and placed the wooden ladle back in the cart and when he turned around, he saw Jesus walking slowly towards him accompanied by Thomas and his father, Abas.

Looking down at Mary, Joseph said, "There he is, Mary!"

As Abas, Jesus, and Thomas approached, Abas, using a tall staff to steady himself, smiled as he waved, "Joseph! Mary!"

"Come and rest a while," Joseph sounded. As Abas sat on the ground Thomas asked, "Father! Would you like a drink of cool water?"

"That would be nice," Abas said as he looked up at Thomas. As Thomas drew some cool water from the cask atop Abas' small cart, Jesus stood silently watching the faces of those passing by wondering what they were thinking. Jesus knew why they had come and what was expected of them as good Jews. They were there for the same reason he and his family was.

Jesus knew that it was mandatory for all male Jews to be in Jerusalem for Passover. Passover was the celebration of freedom and deliverance for the Jews. It was a time of rejoicing for God's miraculous intervention in bringing them out of bondage in Egypt. The celebrating and rejoicing would go on for eight days.

While Joseph, Mary, Abas, and his friend Thomas talked for several minutes, Jesus stared at the crowds and somehow knew it was for them he had been born. And, knowing, now, why he came into the world, we can only assume his heart ached for those who passed; those who were lame, blind, deaf, and mute. His heart must have ached for those who were poor and, and in some cases, even lepers dragging themselves on the ground as people skirted them trying not to get too close.

At this feast of the Passover, Jesus would do all the things a Jew should do, including make sacrifice by offering a pigeon.

It would be a glorious eight days for all those who were there and for all those who were strong and financially able to fulfill their obligations during the celebration.

Then, Jesus felt a hand on his shoulder. He turned about and it was Thomas. "Come, Jesus. We are going into the market place. You do not want to be left behind, do you?"

Chapter III

The Celebration of the Passover

Joseph, Mary, and Jesus spent just about every day with Abas and Thomas. Both Abas and Joseph loved Jerusalem and when they were not worshipping and listening to the stories the priests were telling, they were explaining to the boys why they were the chosen people of God and why sacrificing was so important.

Sitting by their camp fire in the evening, Joseph explained many things to Jesus and his friend, Thomas, as Mary and Abas listened. Joseph explained that blood played an important part at Passover. It was by the blood of the lamb that the people of Israel had been set free from their captivity. At Passover, thousands of unblemished lambs would be taken to the Temple and sold to those who would offer them up as a sacrifice to God.

Each one (the animal being sacrificed) would be carried by three men; one to slit the throat of the animal while the other two assisted. Then, the blood would be collected in basins by priests who would, then, sprinkle it on the altar. In doing this, they were symbolically returning life to God (i.e. the blood which belonged to Him.

*****

The noise of the animals, the chaotic crowds, and the overpowering stench of the blood made the event tiresome. It was no wonder that the men who spent the day in the hot sun, preparing the sacrifice; their robes drenched in blood would be awarded the places of honor at either side of the host at the Passover meal.

Though being in the Temple for the Passover was a festive occasion for all the Jews, it posed a hardship on most of them. One of the first things every Jew who entered the city had to do was to pay a visit to the "moneychangers". These "moneychangers" made huge profits at the expense of the Jews who came to worship and make sacrifice.   Every Jew, whether rich or poor, who had reached the age of twenty was obligated to pay a half shekel as an offering to Jehovah into the Temple's treasury. This offering was to be paid in the exact Hebrew half shekel. At Passover, every male adult who   wanted to worship at the Temple had to bring his offering or purchase a sacrificial animal at the Temple. Because the Temple would not accept any foreign money having any foreign image, the moneychangers would sell Temple money at a very high rate of exchange and assess a fixed charge for their services.

The Temple also had judges who sat and inspected all the offerings to be sacrificed. These judges were very quick to detect any blemishes in the animals that were to be sacrificed. This, of course, was quite expensive for the wealthy Jews, not to mention the hardship it was for the poor who could only offer turtle-doves or pigeons. The priestly authorities took a large percentage on each transaction.

Nevertheless, because most Jews were adamant about their religion, they obeyed the rules and laws and celebrated the Passover, fulfilling their obligations as they should.

The days passed quickly for Joseph, Mary, and Jesus. There was always so much to see and hear and it was difficult for Joseph to try to keep track of where Jesus was most of the time. Jesus had spent a great deal of his time in the evening meeting discussing Scripture with others in the caravan. Joseph and Mary resolved themselves of the fact that if Jesus wasn't in their sight, He was, no doubt, either playing with Thomas and the other children or chatting with others of the caravan who found Him interesting.

So, when Joseph and Mary had done all that was required by the Law of the Lord, they left Jerusalem to return to their own home. When they left, Jesus stayed behind but they were not aware of it. They thought that Jesus was in the company of those in the caravan. He could have been with anyone; Thomas and Abas, a relative, or another friend of the family.

At the end of a day's traveling, because they did not see him, they began looking for him. When it was obvious he wasn't with the caravan, Joseph and Mary returned to Jerusalem to look for Him. After three days, they found Jesus in the Temple courts sitting among the teachers, listening to them and asking them questions. Everyone who heard Jesus was amazed at His understanding, and His answers. When His parents saw Him, they were astonished. Mary said to Him, "Son, why have you treated us like this? Your father and I have been anxiously searching for you."

Jesus responded by saying, "Why were you searching for me? Didn't you know I had to be in my Father's house?" Luke 2: 40-52.

*****

It might have been that those words spoken by Jesus could have reminded Joseph and Mary that the boy they were raising wasn't an ordinary boy. After all, Mary and Joseph knew that Jesus was conceived by the Holy Ghost; or, did they forget? How could they?

When Jesus spoke those words, Mary and Joseph were instantly reminded that Jesus was favored by God. Perhaps they didn't quite comprehend what was going on.

When her son spoke these words, Mary immediately was reminded of that wonderful day she was visited by the Angel Gabriel. (Luke 1: 26-38)

34

The angel said, "Fear not, Mary, for thou hast found grace with God. Behold, thou shalt conceive in thy womb, and shall bring forth a son; and thou shalt call His name Jesus. He shall be called great, and shall be called the Son of the most high; and the Lord shall give unto Him the throne of David, His father; and He shall reign in the house of Jacob forever. And of His kingdom there shall be no end."

So, when Joseph and Mary found Jesus and He spoke these words to them, the anger that was within them immediately vanished since no more concerning their anger was recorded in the Gospels. Joseph and Mary took the child and went home leaving those who heard Him dumbfounded and in awe of His knowledge and wisdom.

*****

Jesus and Thomas remained close friends as they grew. Jesus and Thomas spent many hours during the day hiking and camping. There was one time when He and Thomas were climbing and Thomas fell from a ledge and broke his arm. The pain was excruciating for Thomas as he lie on the ground as Jesus scrambled down the mountain slope to where His friend lay.

Thomas knew he had broken his arm as Jesus approached him. "My arm is broken, Jesus!" Thomas moaned. Thomas was sweating profusely.

Jesus knelt beside his friend and said, "Be still, Thomas." Then, Jesus gently placed his hand on Thomas's arm and the pain immediately disappeared. "There," Jesus said. "Come. Let's go home."

Thomas didn't know what had happened. He just lay on the ground looking up at Jesus. "What did you do, Jesus?" Thomas asked. "Are you some kind of a magician?"

Jesus extended his hand to Thomas and helped him to

35

his feet. Jesus said, "Tell no one of this, Thomas. You will hear and see many wonderful things that cannot be explained. There will be a day when all things can be made known; not only to you but to all who believe in the Son of Man."

The two young men walked, slowly, home and nothing more was said of the incident.

(The Gospels say nothing about Jesus as a young man until He appears later at the Jordan River where He was baptized by the Baptist).

Abas, Thomas's father, sold his land and he and Thomas moved to Jerusalem. Jesus was very sad when this happened.

The two friends rarely got to see each other after Thomas moved. The only times they were able to see each other was if they met in Jerusalem during one of the three holy celebrations.

Abas, being rich, purchased a great deal of land around Bethany and in the Kedron Valley where he and His son Thomas eventually took up residency. Abas later died and Thomas inherited all of his father's wealth which included olive groves and herds of cattle. Thomas married and had children.

While Thomas was busy with his land and family, he often thought about His friend, Jesus.

Jesus, meanwhile, remained in Nazareth and worked as a carpenter with His father until He was about 30 years of age. Joseph died at about this time just before Jesus was to begin His ministry.

Jesus often thought about Thomas and longed to see him again. He knew where His friend was and that he had a family, but, Jesus, being as poor as He was, wasn't able to just go off and stay away. Jesus had to take care of his mother and Joseph and help with the work or they would not be able to survive.

The time came, however, when Jesus had to leave Nazareth and begin His ministry. He was 30 years old, Joseph, his father, had died, and Mary was at least 44 years of age.

When Jesus left home, He might have had a discussion with Mary that went something like this:

Jesus said, "Mother. It is time for me to leave this home and begin the work I came into this world to do."

Mary, who always prayed that the day Jesus would leave would never come, countered, "I do not want you to leave me, my son. But, I know you must." Tears begin to flow from Mary's eyes as she continues. "You are my son, Jesus. I love you and I don't know if I can live without you."

"Do not worry, mother," Jesus said. "I will not leave you alone." He paused, and then added, "You know, I must go, now. But, I will return very shortly and you will always be with me. I will always love you and I will always take care of you."

Mary reached out and hugged her son, and wept, as she said, "Go, my son." Then, she looked into her son's eyes and added, "I must always know where you are. Please come back soon. My place is by your side, Jesus."

"Were I not born for what I must do, I would never go away. But, because I am, it is necessary for me to be about my Father's business." He brushes a tear from His mother's eyes, smiles, and then says, "Do not weep, mother. Be happy and glad that I am sent here for God's purpose. I will come back to you very soon."

Mary smiles, and then concludes, "Hurry back to me, son. I love you."

"I love you, too, mother. Goodbye." Jesus, then, turns

and leaves.

As Jesus leaves the small home, Mary hurries to the door and watches as her son, having only a staff in hand, walks steadily away and out of sight. Mary, no longer waving, lowers her arm and remains in the open door crying.

*****

Mary, of course, had many friends in Nazareth. So, when Jesus left her to do his Father's work, she was not alone. Her husband, Joseph, Jesus' father, was well respected in the community and, having done work for many of the Nazarenes, made many friends who, also, came to know and love Mary. So, when Jesus went away to begin his ministry he knew he did not have to worry about his mother.

Having left Nazareth, Jesus went forth and called at his friend Thomas's home in the Kedron Valley just outside of Jerusalem. He wanted to spend some time with his friend and his family before beginning His ministry.

*****

Thomas saw his friend Jesus coming, staff in hand, and ran to meet him. Jesus, seeing His friend, dropped his staff and the two young men embraced.

"Jesus," Thomas said, all excited as he backed up a few steps to look at his friend. A big smile on his face, Thomas asked, "Where are you going, Jesus? How have you been?"

Jesus picked up His staff and said, "I've come to see *you*, of course."

"How are you? How are your father and your mother?" Thomas asked.

"My mother is fine," Jesus answered.

"And your father; How is he?"

The smile quickly vanished from Jesus' face as he answered, "My father died two months ago."

Seriously, then, Thomas said, "I'm sorry, Jesus. I know how much you loved him."

"Yes," Jesus sounded. "I loved him very much."

Thomas was silent for a few seconds. He, then, put his hand on Jesus' shoulder and said, a smile on his face, "You must be tired and hungry after your long walk. Come and see my wife and children!"

Thomas' wife, Arella, saw her husband and Thomas approaching and welcomed them at the door.

"Arella," Thomas called out. "This is my friend, Jesus, from Nazareth." Thomas introduced, "I want you to meet my wife, Arella."

Jesus smiled and said, "Hello, Arella."

Jesus noticed that Thomas' house was large. It was much larger than the home He, His mother, and Mary, lived in. Thomas, of course, was well to do so he was able to have workers build his home to his specifications.

After they ate, Thomas and Jesus spent hours atop the roof, talking of days gone by while Arella took care of her children and cleaned the dishes.

Most of the homes when Jesus lived had flat roofs where the people who lived would sit and enjoy the evening hours talking and singing. Jesus enjoyed the hours he spent with Thomas. They talked, ate figs, and sipped wine as they reminisced the old days.

But, time was important to Jesus and His stay with Thomas was very brief. The following morning, Jesus said goodbye and was on His way. He knew exactly where He was going.

*****

Jesus on the cross

*****

Chapter IV

Jesus Begins His Ministry
Jesus is baptized by John the Baptist

Chapter III of the Gospel of St. Matthew tells us that in those days, John the Baptist, Jesus' cousin, was preaching in the wilderness of Judea, telling those who came to hear, "Repent, for the Kingdom of Heaven is at hand!"

He wore clothes that were made of camel's hair and had a leather girdle about his waist. His food was locust and wild honey. All those from Jerusalem and Judea, we are told, went out to the Jordan River where John preached and baptized them as they confessed their sins.

Many of the Pharisees and Sadducees came out also to where John was baptizing and he shouted at them saying, "O generation of vipers, who hath warned you to flee from the wrath to come? Bring forth, therefore, fruits and repent!

"And think not to say within yourselves, we have Abraham for our father: for I say unto you, that God is able to from these stones, raise up children unto Abraham.

"And now, also, the ax is laid unto the root of the trees; therefore every tree which bringeth not forth good fruit is hewn down, and cast into the fire.

"I indeed baptize you with water unto repentance; but he that cometh after me is mightier than I, whose shoes I am not worthy to bear; he shall baptize you with the Holy Ghost, and with fire; whose fan is in his hand, and he will thoroughly purge his floor, and gather his wheat into the garner; but he will "burn up the chaff" with unquenchable fire." St. Matthew

*****

(John the Baptist was an extraordinary man. He was an itinerant preacher who lived austerely, challenged sinful rulers, called for repentance, and promised God's justice. Christians commonly refer to John as the precursor forerunner of Jesus).

John was the son of Zachariah, an old man, and his wife, Elisabeth, who was sterile. In the Gospel of Luke, his birth was foretold by the angel Gabriel to Zachariah while Zachariah was performing his functions as a priest in the temple of Jerusalem.

According to Luke, Jesus was conceived when Elisabeth was six months pregnant; when her cousin, the Virgin Mary came to tell her about the news, Elisabeth's unborn child 'jumped for joy' in her womb. Zachariah had lost his speech at the behest and prophecy of the angel Gabriel and it was restored on the occasion of Zachariah naming John.

According to Luke, Jesus and John the Baptist were related, their mothers being cousins; there is, however, no mention of this in any of the other Gospels. (See St. Luke 1:26-38)

Jesus' baptism by John marked the beginning of Jesus' ministry. Both Mark and Luke clearly relate that Jesus came from Galilee to John and was baptized by him, whereupon the Spirit descended upon Him, and a voice from Heaven told Him He was God's Son. John, notably, is thought of as the last prophet.

Jesus came to the Jordan River where John was baptizing when he was about 30 years old. Because people came from miles around, it had to be a hectic scene when He arrived.

When John was baptizing, the water was clean and pure, not like it is today. Today, by all accounts, the place where Jesus was baptized is polluted. Quasar al-Yehuda, a few kilometers from where the river spills into the Dead Sea and just south of the Allenby Bridge has drawn over 100,000 tourists a year. Most of them Christian pilgrims who want to undergo baptism there. It is venerated as the most likely place where John the Baptist baptized Jesus and declared Him the Messiah.

But drought and diversion for irrigation have turned the lower Jordan River into a stagnant stream as it makes its way from the Sea of Galilee. The brook then swells with raw sewage as it passes Jericho. Officials from the Health Ministry said they have demanded that the Nature and Parks Authority take samples of the baptismal waters for testing, but they have yet to receive the results.

"And then cometh Jesus from Galilee to Jordan, unto John, to be baptized of him. But John forbad him saying, "I have need to be baptized of thee."

"Suffer it to be so now: for thus it becometh us to fulfill all righteousness." Then he suffered him.

And Jesus, when He was baptized, went up straightway out of the water: and, lo, the heavens were opened unto Him, and He saw the Spirit of God descending like a dove, and lighting upon Him: And lo a voice from heaven, saying, This is my beloved Son, in whom I am well pleased." (Matt. 3:13-17)

Then was Jesus led up of the Spirit into the wilderness to be tempted of the devil. And when he had fasted forty days and forty nights, he was afterward a hungered. And when the tempter came to him, he said, "if thou be the Son of God, command that these stones be made bread."

But he answered and said, "It is written, man shall not live by bread alone, but by every word that proceeds out of the mouth of God."

Then the devil taketh him up into the holy city, and

setteth him on a pinnacle of the temple, And saith unto him, "If thou be the Son of God, cast thyself down: for it is written, He shall give his angels charge concerning thee: and in *their* hands they shall bear thee up, lest at any time thou dash thy foot against a stone.".

Jesus said unto him, it is written again, "Thou shalt not tempt the Lord thy God."

Again, the devil taketh him up into an exceeding high mountain, and sheweth him all the kingdoms of the world, and the glory of them; and saith unto him, "All these things will I give thee, if thou wilt fall down and worship me."

Then saith Jesus unto him, "get thee hence, Satan: for it is written, Thou shalt worship the Lord thy God, and Him only shalt thou serve." Then the devil leaveth Him, and, behold, angels came and ministered unto Him.

Verse 17 of St. Matthew tells us that from that time on Jesus began to preach saying, "Repent, for the kingdom of heaven is at hand!"

Jesus chose disciples that would follow Him. He would teach them what He wanted them to know and show them all He wanted them to see. The first two disciples to be chosen were Andrew and Peter. After that, He chose two who were brothers; they were James and John. These four disciples were fishermen at the Sea of Galilee.

Jesus called the above and, in doing so, told them to "follow me and I will make you fishers of men."

Later came James, the son of Alphaeus, Phillip, Bartholomew (Nathaniel), Thomas, Matthew, Judas Iscariot, and Simon the Zealot, and Thaddeus.

Before Jesus had decided on the above 12, even though He felt from the start of His ministry that these were those who would be with Him constantly, listen to all He said, and be witness to all He would do, He slipped away one night and went to a nearby mountain and prayed all night. You see, Jesus had many friends, and others, as well as the 12 mentioned above, who wanted to be His constant companion and wanted to learn from Him.

After He had finished praying, He returned to His friends and all those who were with Him and made His decision final. First, Simon (who is called Peter) and his brother Andrew; James son of Zebedee, and his brother John; Philip and Bartholomew; Thomas and Matthew the tax collector; James son of Alphaeus, and Thaddeus, Simon the Zealot, and Judas Iscariot who betrayed him. The Bible also lists the twelve disciples/apostles in Mark 3:16-19.

The word apostle comes from the same Greek word as missionary, and means a sent one. The twelve apostles stayed with him all the time after this, he was their teacher and they were his pupils. He was training them for the work they must do after He would leave them. So he taught them about himself, about his heavenly Father, and the kingdom of heaven.

St. John's Gospel, Chapter 1 gives a different account of how Jesus met those who would be His disciples/apostles. If we read St. John, Chapter 1, we are told that, the day following Jesus' baptism, Jesus was "passing by" as John stood watching with two of his disciples. As Jesus passed by, the Baptist said, "Behold, the Lamb of God." Then, we are told, the two disciples turned, left the Baptist, and followed after Jesus.

When Jesus saw the two men following after Him, He turned and asked, "What seek ye?"

Andrew spoke saying, "Rabbi, where do you dwell?" (The word "rabbi" means master or teacher).

"Come and see," Jesus said. The two went with Jesus

and stood with him for the entire day.

Jesus must have astonished the two young men because, later, Andrew, whose brother was Simon, a fisherman, and aboard (Messiah, interpreted, means the "Christ") his boat when Andrew saw him, shouted, "We have found the Messiah

When Simon, Andrew's brother, heard that "we have found the Messiah!" he must have felt bothered because he knew of his brothers activities with John the Baptist and, probably, told him lots of times that he found the Messiah. Besides, Simon was a hard-working man. He had his own boat and had responsibilities. He was a married man and he had children, and debt.

The first words from Simon's mouth might have been, "Again? I thought you found the messiah last month. Can't you see I'm busy?"

"But, you've got to come with me and meet this man. He is unlike any other I've heard. You've got to come with me and listen to this man speak!"

Andrew had to be very persistent because Simon Peter finally threw up his hands and agreed to go with Andrew to meet Jesus. He might have said something like, "Alright, Andrew. But this is the last time I'm going to give in. After this, I'll expect you to come and help me on the boat. This nonsense about you finding the messiah every couple of months is getting ridiculous!"

"OK, but come. You must listen to this man speak. I know He *is* the messiah!"

Reluctantly, Simon went with Andrew to meet Jesus. And, when Jesus saw Simon, He said, "Thou art Simon, the son of Jonah; thou shalt be called Cephas," which is by interpretation, a stone.

Jesus later chose those who would be with him always,

as mentioned above. Being with Jesus, they were direct witnesses to the miracles He performed which included raising the dead. His first miracle was the changing of water into wine in Capernaum. Jesus and His disciples were invited to a wedding. It can be said that this wedding was the first Christian wedding on record.

The incident is recorded in the Gospel according to St. John Verses 1-11. Jesus and His disciples were seated having a good time when Mary, the mother of Jesus, said to Him, "Jesus, they have no wine."

Looking first at his companions, and then at Mary, Jesus asked, "Woman, what has this to do with me? My hour has not yet come." (Notice here that Jesus calls His mother, woman. This, of course was not meant to show disrespect. It was simply the manner in which they spoke in those days. Also, Jesus might have thought, at that time, that those in charge should have planned ahead so they would not run out of wine, or anything else. Besides, Mary might have approached Jesus because they could have been relatives and assumed that her son, Jesus, would have wanted to help in some way).

The fact that Jesus might have been a bit annoyed by his mother's plea for help could be inferred because He remarked that "my hour has not yet come". He could have had it on his mind that He did not want to reveal his Godly powers just for the sake of a lot of people having wine to drink at a wedding reception in Cana.

Nevertheless, Jesus loved Mary and wanted to make her happy. He decided to act on her request. Jesus, then, stood and followed his mother to where the servants stood next to the empty wine casks. As they approached the servants, Mary spoke to them, saying, "Whatever He tells you to do, do it."

47

"Bring me six water pots of stone, each holding 20 or 30 gallons of water," Jesus said. The servants did as Jesus commanded as the disciples, and others watched.

After Jesus made sure the water pots were filled to the brim, Jesus remarked, "he that drinks from this water shall thirst again."

After the guests tasted the wine, the governor of the feast, that is to say, he who was in charge, said, "Every man at the beginning set forth good wine, and when men have well drunk, they would put forth the inferior wine. But," he added, "Thou hast kept the good wine until now."

"Beginning of miracles did Jesus in Cana of Galilee, and manifested forth His glory: and His disciples believed on Him." Nothing like this has ever been said of the miracles of the prophets or apostles."

★★★★★

Chapter V

Jesus Challenges the Moneychangers in the Temple
Many Believe in Jesus

Jesus Christ came to the earth and, we all know, had a very definite mission. His mission was not to perform miracles. "I have come that they might have life, and have it more abundantly." (John 10:10b) Plainly put, Jesus came to the earth to restore to mankind what was lost because of Adam's disobedience. He came to offer to mankind a means of reconciliation with God, the Father, so that when man's life on Earth was ended, he might live again, everlastingly. This is what God intended when He created Adam and placed him in the Garden of Eden.

Luke 19:10 tells us, Jesus said, "I have come to seek and to save that which was lost." And finally: Jesus said, "For I have come down from heaven, not to do my own will, but the will of Him who sent me. This is the will of the Father who sent me, that of all He has given me I should lose nothing, but should raise it up at the last day. And this is the will of Him who sent me; that everyone who sees the Son and believes in Him may have everlasting life; and I will raise him up at the last day." (John 6:35-40)

*****

After the wedding, Jesus said, "Come, let us go to Jerusalem." There they would attend the Feast of the Passover. When Jesus and His disciples arrived, they went through the gate and Jesus stopped abruptly. When He looked around, He thought He was in the midst of what appeared to be an auction. He might have thought to Himself, "What is this? Is this an auction on the temple grounds?"

He looked and saw that oxen, sheep, doves, and other

49

livestock were being auctioned off. "What's going on here?" Jesus might have said to Himself. He could plainly see that money was changing hands and that business was being done, for profit, right in plain view. And, it was being done right in the holy temple in Jerusalem. Jesus was angry and appalled. He looked at His disciples and hollered, "How can they defile God's Holy Temple? This is disgraceful and I will not permit it!"

The disciples were astonished to see that Jesus would carry on so when He had known since he first visited the temple with His father and Mary many years before that the temple was all about making a profit. Jesus was well aware of the fact that the temple was making huge profits exchanging money and selling animals to be sacrificed. So, why, now, was Jesus putting on such a show of anger?

Perhaps because He was only beginning His ministry, and expressing His anger against the money changers in the temple would most certainly be one way for the people to take notice of Him. Another reason, in my opinion, was because the money changers and the profit they made by exchanging foreign money into shekels to be used to purchase animals for sacrifice was, no doubt, on Jesus' mind. Jesus, being God, knew that *He* had come to be a *human* sacrifice for man's sins and it might have been His way of expressing anger at them; and how they used the people to believe that they were "appeasing" his Father.

In the Gospel of St. John, Chap. 2:13-16, we learn that Jesus created a whip using some cords and He began using it to drive away the money changers, along with the sheep and oxen as He overturned the tables yelling, "Get out of here! You have made my father's house a house of merchandise!"

In the Gospel of St. Matthew 21: 12-13, as Jesus was

casting the moneychangers out of the temple, He said, "It is written, my house shall be called the house of prayer, but you have made it a den of thieves!"

The synoptic gospels, and John, state that Jesus left the temple after the incident with the money changers, but returned to the Temple courts a day later (though Luke is unspecific how many days had passed), and begins teaching. (The Gospels of Matthew, Mark, and Luke are known as the synoptic gospels because they include many of the same stories, often in the same sequence, and sometimes exactly the same wording. This degree of parallelism in content, narrative arrangement, language, and sentence structures can only be accounted for by literary interdependence. Most scholars believe that these gospels share the same point of view and are clearly linked. The term synoptic comes from the Greek *syn*, meaning "together", and *optic*, meaning "seen"). Apocryphal gospels, as well as the canonical Gospel of John, differ greatly from the Synoptic Gospels.

After Jesus had driven the money changers out of the temple, the priests, teachers, and the elders screamed to Jesus, "What gives you the right to do this?" some asked. Others questioned, asking, "Who do you think you are?"

Jesus snapped back, saying, "How dare you use the house of God to turn it into a marketplace! It is all of *you* who defile the house of God!"

The Jews then said to Him, 'What sign can you show us for doing this?'

Jesus answered them, "Destroy this temple, and in three days I will raise it up."

The Jews then said, "This temple has been under construction for forty-six years, and will you raise it up in three days?"

But Jesus was speaking of the temple of His body. (After He was raised from the dead, His disciples remembered that He had said this; and they believed the scripture and the word that Jesus had spoken). (Gospel of St. John Chapter 2)

Jesus in the Temple

It is clear that when Jesus said, "Destroy this temple, and in three days I will raise it up," He was referring to the resurrection. The Jews scolded Jesus asking "show us a sign!"

Jesus' response that the temple, if destroyed, would rise in three days was, apparently, confusing to them. They never surmised that when Jesus said this, He was speaking of Himself as the Temple that would, once they killed Him, rise again (come back to life). Surely, once they would see this happen, it would be such a "sign" that they *would* believe Him to be The Son of Man. Simply put Jesus was saying that in three days *I* will live again if you kill me. And, when he would arise, they will surely know He is the Son of God, with power, that had power of laying down His life, and taking it up again; and this is the very sign; namely, His resurrection from the dead on the third day, (this sign that) He gives the Jews, when they sought Him at another time, and upon another occasion.

The last couple of verses of Chap. 2 in St. John tell us that when the Jews saw the signs that Jesus did, many believed in Him. So, what were the signs the Gospel writer was talking about that Jesus did that caused "many" to believe?

When John wrote that Jesus caused many to believe, He was not writing of the things the Lord had done, then, and at that specific time. He was writing to say that all the things Jesus had done over the course of His ministry were the reasons that many believed. John, as I interpret the scripture, has inferred that Jesus had given the Jews the greatest sign of all in stating, "Destroy this Temple and in three days it would rise again." Because, in making this statement, Jesus is referring to the resurrection, which, in essence, is what the gospel is all about.

(From here on, I am using the Gospel of St. John as my reference in the writing of this work).

I cannot continue this book without going into detail concerning those who ruled the Jews, namely, the ruling class. I must explain because Jesus was in constant conflict with them. I will point out, briefly, the sects/religions that made up the ruling class during Jesus' ministry. The ruling classes at that time were made up of Pharisees, the Sadducees, and some who might have been, at one time or another, members of the Essenes.

The first surviving historical mention of the *Pharisees* is from the Jewish-Roman historian Josephus (37–100 CE), in a description of the "four schools of thought," or "four sects," into which the Jews were divided in the 1st century BCE; the other schools were the Essenes, who were generally apolitical and who may have emerged as a sect of dissident priests who rejected either the Seleucid-appointed or the Hasmonean high priests as illegitimate; the Sadducees, who were the main antagonists of the Pharisees; and the "fourth philosophy" possibly associated with the anti-Roman revolutionary groups such as the Sicarii and the Zealots. Other sects emerged at this time, such as the Early Christians in Jerusalem and the Therapeutic in Egypt.

The book 2 Maccabees, which in the Christian tradition

is a <u>deuterocanonical</u> book of the <u>Bible</u>, focuses on the <u>Jews'</u> revolt against <u>Antiochus IV Epiphanes</u> and concludes with the defeat of the <u>Syrian</u> General <u>Nicanor</u> in 161 BCE by <u>Judas Maccabeus</u>, the <u>hero</u> of the work. It was likely written by a Pharisee or someone sympathetic toward Pharisees, as it includes several theological innovations: propitiatory prayer for the dead, judgment day, intercession of saints, and merits of the martyrs. <u>The Mishnah</u> is an authoritative codification of Pharisaic law, edited by <u>Judah haNasi</u> around 200 CE. Most of the authorities quoted in the Mishnah lived after the destruction of the Temple in 70 CE; it thus marks the beginning of the transition from Pharisaic to Rabbinic (i.e. modern normative) Judaism. (I have decided not to go into a lengthy overview of Jewish History and Religion).

Unlike the Sadducees, the Pharisees also believed in the <u>resurrection of the dead</u> in a future, messianic age. The Pharisees believed in a literal resurrection of the body. (See below)

According to Josephus, whereas the Sadducees believed that people have total <u>free will</u> and the Essenes believed that all of a person's life is <u>predestined</u>, the Pharisees believed that people have free will but that God also has foreknowledge of human <u>destiny</u>. According to Josephus, Pharisees were further distinguished from the Sadducees in that Pharisees believed in the <u>resurrection of the dead</u>; the Sadducees did not.

The *Sadducees* (<u>Hebrew</u>: צדוקים Tzedukim) were a sect or group of Jews that were active in Ancient Israel during the <u>Second Temple period</u>, starting from the 2nd century BC through the destruction of the Temple in 70 AD.

The sect was identified by <u>Josephus</u> with the upper social and economic echelon of Judean society. As a whole, the sect fulfilled various political, social and religious roles, including maintaining the Temple. The Sadducees are often compared to other contemporaneous sects, including the Pharisees, the Essenes, and the Early Christian movement. Their sect is believed to have become extinct sometime after the destruction of Herod's Temple in Jerusalem in 70 AD, but it has been speculated that later Karaits may have had some roots or connections with old Sadducee views (Hebrew: צדוקים Tzedukim) were a sect or group of Jews that were active in Ancient Israel during the Second Temple period, starting from the 2nd century BC through the destruction of the Temple in 70 AD. (Source of information includes Wikipedia.org).

So, when Jesus was carrying on with His ministry, those who ruled were the Pharisees and the Sadducees. Josephus, one of the best known writers of Jewish Antiquity who lived during the first century was also a Pharisee.

And, who were the Essenes? There is much to be said about the Essenes. The main source of information concerning this sect comes from Wikipedia.org. and etc. including my own formal education.

Josephus gave a detailed account of the Essenes in *The Jewish War* (c. 75 A.D.), with a shorter description in *Antiquities of the Jews* (c. 94 A.D.) and The Life of Flavius Josephus (c. 97 A.D.). Claiming first-hand knowledge, he lists the *Essenoi* as one of the three sects of Jewish philosophy alongside the Pharisees and the Sadducees. He relates the same information concerning piety, celibacy, the absence of personal property, and of money, the belief in communality and commitment to a strict observance of the Sabbath. He further adds that the Essenes ritually immersed in water every morning, ate together after prayer, devoted themselves to charity and benevolence, forbade the expression of anger, studied the books of the elders, preserved secrets, and were very mindful of the names of the angels kept in their sacred writings.

The accounts by Josephus and Philo show that the Essenes led a strictly <u>celibate</u> and <u>communal</u> life – often compared by scholars to later <u>Christian</u> <u>monastic</u> living – although Josephus speaks also of another *"order* of Essenes" that observed being engaged for three years and then being married. According to Josephus, they had customs and observances such as collective ownership, elected a leader to attend to the interests of them all whose orders they obeyed, were forbidden from <u>swearing oaths</u> and <u>sacrificing animals</u>, controlled their temper and served as channels of peace, carried <u>weapons</u> only as protection against robbers, had no <u>slaves</u> but served each other, and, as a result of communal ownership, did not engage in <u>trading</u>. Both Josephus and Philo have lengthy accounts of their communal meetings, meals and religious celebrations.

(I feel it is also necessary for me to briefly describe "Zealot"). The name Zealot was used to describe a member of a group of Jewish rebels who attempted the military overthrow of Roman rule in Palestine in the 1st and 2nd centuries AD. Zealot was formed from the word zeal, which is enthusiasm for a particular cause. The related adjective zealous means "enthusiastic and full of zeal." One of Jesus' followers had been a Zealot prior to becoming one of the 12 apostles. His name was Simon.

★★★★★

Chapter VI

Nicodemus Speaks with Jesus
Jesus and the Woman of Samaria

The Gospel of St. John goes on to tell us that there was a man named Nicodemus who was a Pharisee. Nicodemus said, "We know that thou art a teacher sent from God for no man can do the miracle you do except God be with him."

Jesus looked at Nicodemus and responded by saying, "Except a man be born again he cannot see the Kingdom of God."

Nicodemus, a confused look on his face, questioned, "How can a man be born when he is old? Can he enter a second time into his mother's womb and be born?"

Jesus answered, "Except a man be born of water and of spirit he cannot enter into the Kingdom of God." Using a convincing tone, He continued, "Marvel not that I tell you that you must be born again. The wind blows to where it is but you don't know where it came from or where it is going: so is everyone who is born of the Spirit."

Scratching his head, a confused Nicodemus questions, "But, how can this be?"

"You are a master of Israel and yet you do not know these things?" Jesus said. "Verily, verily, I say unto thee, we speak that we do know, and testify that we have seen; and ye receive not our witness. If I have told you earthly things, and ye believe not, how shall ye believe, if I tell you *of* heavenly things? And no man hath ascended up to heaven, but He that came down from heaven, *even* the Son of man which is in heaven. For God so loved the world, that he gave his only begotten Son, that whosoever believeth in him should not perish, but have everlasting life. For God sent not his Son into the world to condemn the world; but that the world through him might be saved. He that believeth on him is not condemned: but he that believeth not is condemned already, because he hath not believed in the name of the only begotten Son of God. And this is the condemnation, that light is come into the world, and men loved darkness rather than light, because their deeds were evil. For every one that doeth evil hateth the light, neither cometh to the light, lest his deeds should be reproved. But he that doeth truth cometh to the light that his deeds may be made manifest, that they are wrought in God." Nicodemus turned and Jesus watched him slowly leave.

Shortly thereafter, Jesus and His disciples went into the land of Judaea and, the Bible tells us, there He tarried and baptized. But, we learn later in St. John 4:2 that Jesus never baptized anyone. His disciples did the baptizing. (Judaea is the land that surrounds Jerusalem).

John's Gospel is here distinguishing the city of Jerusalem from Judaea informing us that Jesus left the city and went into the countryside. We later learn that Jesus spent more time in the country side and traveled from village to village performing miracles and teaching.

*****

John the Baptist was also baptizing near Salim and the people came and were baptized. John, up until now, had not yet been put in prison.

Some of his disciples approached Him and said to him, "Rabbi, He who was with you beyond the Jordan, to whom ye bore witness, here He is, baptizing, and the people are going to Him."

John answered, "No one can receive anything except what is given him from heaven. You, yourselves, bear me witness that I said, I am not the Christ, but I have been sent before Him. He who has the bride is the bridegroom; the friend of the bridegroom who stands and hears him rejoices greatly at the bridegroom's voice; therefore," John continues, "this joy of mine is now full. He must increase, but I must decrease."

John, now, deep in thought, looks towards the heavens, and then, again, at those who were with Him. He says, "He who comes from heaven is above all. For He whom God has sent speaks the words of God, for it is not by measure that He gives the Spirit; the Father loves the Son, and has given all things into his hand. He who believes in the Son has eternal life; he who does not obey the Son shall not see life, but the wrath of God rests upon him."

*****

Jesus later traveled into Samaria with His disciples and stopped at a well where, and soon, a woman came to draw water. Normally, Jesus would have traveled around Samaria so as to avoid going through Samaria. Jesus, however, didn't want to lose time so He went directly to a Town called Sychar, which was near Jacob's well. He had already sent His disciples to the city to buy food.

*****

(Here, I will refer you to the history behind why the Jews and the Samaritans had such enmity between them).

From the time of the division of Israel that began at around 930 BC, after the death of King Solomon, the ten tribes of the Northern Kingdom, and the two tribes, Judah and Benjamin, of the Southern Kingdom, waged intermittent wars with each other for about the next two centuries. The Northern Kingdom is generally referred to as Israel, and the Southern Kingdom was referred to as Judah.

(To learn the history concerning the division of the Israel Nation in its entirety, go to: http://davcarson.home.mindspring.com and reference Intertestamental/Samaritan). The story involved would take too much time and it would be necessary for me to prepare a book to properly relate the matter).

*****

It was about noon and Jesus, sitting, wiping His forehead, said to the woman, "Give me a drink."

"You are a Jew," she said, "and I am a Samaritan woman. Why do you ask me for a drink?" She knew that the Jews want nothing to do with the Samaritans.

Jesus responded by saying, "If you knew the gift of God and who it is that is asking you for a drink, you would have asked Him and He would have given you living water."

"But, sir," the woman said, "you have nothing to draw with and the well is deep." Then, she thought and, asked quizzically, "where can I get this living water? Are you greater than our Father Jacob who gave us the well and drank from it himself, as did also his sons and livestock?"

"Woman," Jesus said, "Everyone who drinks this water will thirst again. The water I will give them will never thirst again. The water I will give them will become in them a spring of water welling up to eternal life."

Almost pleading, the woman said, "Sir, give me this water so I won't thirst and have to keep coming here to draw water."

Quickly, Jesus said, "Go and call your husband and come back!"

"I have no husband," the woman said.

"You were right in saying you have no husband. You have had five husbands, and the man you have now is not your husband. It is good you spoke the truth."

"I can see you are a prophet," said the woman." Then, in an attempt to justify, ever so briefly, why the Samaritans worshipped how and where they did, stated, "Our ancestors worshipped on this mountain, but you Jews claim that we must worship in Jerusalem."

With a faint smile on His face, Jesus replied, "Woman, the time will come when you will worship the Father neither on this mountain nor in Jerusalem. You Samaritans worship what you do not know; we worship what we do know, for salvation is from the Jews. Yet a time is coming and now has come when the true worshippers will worship the Father in the Spirit, and in truth, for they are the kind of worshippers the Father seeks. God is Spirit and they that worship Him must worship Him in Spirit and in truth."

"I know the Messiah (the Christ) is coming. When He does come," the woman said, "He will explain everything to us."

Then Jesus declared, "I, He who is speaking to you, am He."

Jesus openly declared that He was the Messiah.

Just then, the disciples returned but not one of them asked Jesus what they had talked about.

The woman left Jesus and told those in her town of Him. Many returned and believed in Jesus, and He tarried there for two days before leaving for Galilee.

*****

When Jesus had come into Galilee, He was welcomed because, having seen all He had done in Jerusalem at the feast, they, too, had gone to the feast. And, He went into Cana where He changed the water into wine. Then, in Capernaum, there was an official whose son was very ill. When the official heard that Jesus had come from Judea to Galilee, he went and begged Him to go with him and heal his son, for his son was near death.

"Sir," the official said, "Come down before my son dies!"

Then, Jesus said, "Go; your son will live."

The man believed what Jesus told him and, while on his way to his house, his servants met him and told him that his son was living. He asked his servants the hour when his son began to get well. They told him, "Yesterday, the seventh hour, your son began to get well when the fever left him." The official knew that that was the hour Jesus said his son will live. And, because of this, he and his entire family believed in Jesus. This was the second sign that Jesus did when He came from Judea into Galilee.

After this, there was a feast of the Jews and Jesus went back into Jerusalem.

St. John tells us that there is in Jerusalem by the "Sheep Gate" a pool. In Hebrew it is called Bethesda, having five porticos. In these porticos lay a multitude of invalids; those who were blind, lame, paralyzed, and even lepers. One man was there who had been ill for thirty eight years. When Jesus saw him and knew he had been lying there for a very long time, He asked him, "Do you want to be healed?"

The man answered Him, "Sir, I have no-one to help me into the pool when the water is troubled, and while I am struggling to get in, another steps in before me."

Jesus said, "Rise, take up your pallet and walk!" The man was healed instantly. The day Jesus did this was the Sabbath.

The Jews said to the man, "It is the Sabbath; it is not lawful for you to carry your pallet."

The man replied, "But, the man who healed me told me to pick up my pallet and walk."

The Jews asked him, "Who was it that told you to pick

up your pallet and walk?"

But the man did not know who it was who healed him so he could not tell those who questioned him. Afterwards, Jesus found the man in the temple and said to him, "You see, you are well! Sin no more that nothing worse befall you."

The man went away and told the Jews that it was Jesus who healed him. The Jews persecuted Jesus because He healed on the Sabbath.

But Jesus replied, "My Father is working even now as I am working, still." This was why the Jews sought to kill Jesus. Because He not only broke the Sabbath, He called God His Father making Himself equal with God.

Jesus continued, saying, "Truly, truly, I say to you, the Son can do nothing on His own but only what He sees the Father doing; for whatever the Father does, the Son will do likewise. The Father loves the Son and shows Him all He Himself is doing. And, greater works than these will He show Him, that you may marvel. For as the Father raises the dead and gives them life, so will the Son of Man give life to whomever He will. The Father judges no one, but has given all judgment to the Son so that all may honor the Son, even as they honor the Father.

"He who does not honor the Son does not honor the Father who sent Him. I tell you," Jesus said, "he who hears my word and believes Him who sent me will have eternal life; he who does not come into judgment, but has passed from death to life.

"I tell you this; the hour is coming, and now is, when the dead will hear the voice of the Son of God, and all those who hear will live. For as the Father has life in Himself; so, He has granted the Son to also have life in Himself and has given Him authority to carry out judgment because He is the Son of Man."

Jesus paused a second or two as He noticed the reactions those who were listening displayed. Then, He added, "Do not marvel at what I say. The hour is coming when all who are in the tombs will hear His voice and come forth; those who have done good to the resurrection of life, and those who have done evil to the resurrection of the judgment. I can do nothing on my own," Jesus said. "As I hear, I judge; and, my judgment is just because I seek not my own will but the will of He who sent me."

"If I bear witness to myself, my testimony is not true; there is another who bears witness to me, and I know that the testimony which he bears to me is true. You sent to John, and he has borne witness to the truth. Not that the testimony which I receive is from man; but I say this that you may be saved. He was a burning and shining lamp, and you were willing to rejoice for a while in his light. But the testimony which I have is greater than that of John; for the works which the Father has granted me to accomplish, these very works which I am doing, bear me witness that the Father has sent me. And the Father who sent me has himself borne witness to me. His voice you have never heard, his form you have never seen; and you do not have his word abiding in you, for you do not believe him whom he has sent. You search the scriptures because you think that in them you have eternal life; and it is they that bear witness to me; yet you refuse to come to me that you may have life.

"I do not receive glory from men. But I know that you have not the love of God within you. I have come in my Father's name, and you do not receive me; if another comes in his own name, him you will receive. How can you believe, who receive glory from one another and do not seek the glory that comes from the only God? Do not think that I shall accuse you to the Father; it is Moses who accuses you, on whom you set your hope. If you believed Moses, you would believe me, for he wrote of me. But if you do not believe his writings, how will you believe my words?" (Read St. John Chapter 5 in its entirety).

*****

Paul's conversion on the Road to Damascus

*****

Chapter VII
Jesus Feeds 5000 People
Jesus Walks on the Water

After these things Jesus went over the Sea of Galilee, which is *the sea* of Tiberias. And a great multitude followed Him, because they saw His miracles which He did on them that were diseased. And Jesus went up into a mountain, and there He sat with His disciples. (Here, John makes mention of the fact the Feast of the Passover was nigh).

Jesus and his disciples were very tired so they sat down. The Lord closed His eyes for a few seconds and, when He opened them, saw that a great multitude had followed Him. They had come, of course, to hear His words, and many had come expecting a miracle.

Then Jesus asked Philip, "When shall we buy bread so we can feed the people?" Jesus, of course, knew what He would do. And, He knew what Philip would say in response to His question.

Philip said, "We can only purchase two hundred pennyworth of bread and that would not be sufficient even if every-one of them takes a little." (According to the Currency Fact Sheets on www.GFT.com, In William Smith's *A Bible Dictionary, rev. ed.* (1948) it says, "Two hundred pennyworth of bread would have cost approximately thirty-two dollars." So considering inflation (2010), it's about 282 dollars. Read more: http://wiki.answers.com/Q/How_much_is_two_hundred_pe nnyworth_in_US_currency#ixzz1NZRNNUj7).

Jesus knew that they didn't have enough money to purchase the amount of food needed to feed such a multitude of people. The Gospel of John tells us there were some 5,000 people that had to be fed. Jesus sat, waiting, to hear what his disciples would say concerning the matter.

He had a smile on His face as He sat waiting for them to express themselves.

Just then, Andrew, Simon Peter's brother, stood and said, "There is a lad here with 5 barley loaves and two small fishes." He paused and using his right hand to scratch his head, continued. "But, what are they among so many?"

Jesus had heard enough. He sighed deeply and said to His disciples, "Make those who are here sit down and bring me the lad and the 5 loaves and 2 fish. So Jesus took the loaves and the fish and, after blessing and giving thanks for that which the lad offered, distributed the food to the disciples. They, then, distributed to the 5,000 who had come to hear Jesus.

And all those who were there ate and were filled. And when the 5,000 were filled, Jesus instructed the disciples to, "Gather up that which is left so nothing is wasted."

And, the disciples gathered together 12 baskets filled with what was left of the 5 barley loaves over and above that which was eaten by the multitude. And those who witnessed this event, said, "This is of a truth the prophet that should come into the world." All they that were there were amazed.

They were so amazed that Jesus surmised that they would come and take Him by force to make Him king. So, He left and went atop a nearby mountain, alone, and prayed for a long time. And, He concentrated on what His mission was. And because He was a man, also, must have thought about the pain and suffering He was going to have to endure. He, no doubt, thought about His mother, Mary, and Joseph, His father, and the many wonderful times they had together. For, He truly loved his mother and father.

And, possibly, He thought about the terrific times He and His friend Thomas had when they were children.

A smile came to Jesus' face when He thought about how He and His friend Thomas used to tease the girls. The idea that Jesus is the Son of God and understood by all Christian denominations to be God, as is Jehovah, and the Holy Spirit, is all the more wonderful that He, though God, was man, also.

And, only because Jesus is/was both God and man, was He able to carry out His mission for the salvation of all mankind. Again, had Jesus not experienced suffering, pain, and death, His sacrifice would have been meaningless. He had to be as a man to experience life as a man and overcome Satan and the temptations of the devil as man is asked to do. And, since He was able to overcome Satan, He became the perfect sacrifice for the salvation of all mankind. Thus, by the shedding of His blood He was, as a man, able to pay the price and reconcile man to God, as a man.

So, Jesus experienced life as a man and because his life was so exemplary, He was the only one worthy of the task for which He came into the world. He lived among men, as a man, for the purpose of accomplishing that which He had come into the world to accomplish. But, before He was a man, he was a child. And, as a child, He behaved as a child, and did the things children do. They go to school, they learn, they play, and, at times, do things that are annoying to adults, and appear rowdy. Jesus was, although different from other children in many ways, was like any other child in many other ways.

Jesus smiled when He thought about how he and his friend Thomas used to tease certain girls. One time, Thomas became a bit too rowdy and began pulling on Yaffa's hair. He just wouldn't let up. Yaffa (The name in Hebrew means beautiful) began crying and ran home after which her mother came, scolding Thomas and threatening to tell his father.

"Why do you do that?" Jesus asked Thomas.

"I don't know!" Thomas replied. "It's fun, I guess."

"You're not going to think its so much fun when your father finds out!" Jesus said.

"Aw," Thomas said. "Come on! Let's go climbing."

Jesus smiled when He thought about the things He and Thomas did when they were children. But, shrugging his shoulders, Jesus probably thought to himself, "That's what kids do." And, Jesus did what lots of kids did. But, the wonderful thing about all of this is that He is God and, yet, He became flesh and dwelt among us as one of us.

When Jesus was able to get away from the crowds, He often thought about these things. Then He would pray as we should; asking God the Father to direct our paths. His time alone was always short before He would be interrupted by one of his disciples or someone seeking help.

When night time came, the disciples went down into the sea. That is to say; the disciples got into a ship and sailed toward Capernaum. Up to this time, Jesus, we are told, had not yet come to them. And, then there was a great wind that began to toss the disciples about; and the ship, also. And the disciples began to fear for their lives.

They had gone about 25 – 30 furlongs and then noticed Jesus coming towards them, walking on the water (A furlong is approximately an eighth of a mile). Jesus said, "It is I! Don't be afraid!" The disciples, then, helped Jesus into the ship and they continued until they reached "the other side."

The following day those that were there were astonished to see Jesus knowing He had not departed with his disciples and nor with others who were on the other side. Because they had not seen another boat, they were in awe that Jesus had gotten over the sea, and were full of wonder. When some began to question the Lord, He replied, "Ye seek me, not because of the miracles, but because ye did eat of the loaves and were filled." He continued, "Labour not for meat that perishes but for that meat which endureth unto everlasting life, which the Son of Man shall give to you."

They asked Jesus, "What shall we do that we might work the works of God?"

Jesus replied, "Ye must believe in Him, "Ye must believe in Him whom the Father hath sent. Our fathers did eat manna in the desert," Jesus said. "As it is written, he gave them bread from heaven to eat. Verily, verily, I say unto you, Moses gave you not that bread from heaven, but my Father gives you the true bread from heaven. For, the bread of God is he which came down from heaven to give life unto the world."

And, they pleaded with him, saying, "Lord, give us this bread."

Jesus, then, made all things clear to the multitude by saying, "I am the bread which came down from heaven to give life unto the world."

Still, the multitude did not understand for they implored Jesus, "Lord, give us this bread!"

"I am the bread of life," Jesus said, emphatically. "He that cometh to me shall never hunger. And, he that believeth on me shall never thirst... he that cometh to me, I shall in no wise cast out."

Jesus sighed softly, and then added, "I came down from heaven not to do my own will, but to do the will of him that sent me. And this is the Father's will which hath sent me; that everyone that sees the Son, and believes in him, may have everlasting life; and I will raise him up at the last day."

The Jews, now, began to murmur amongst themselves, because of the things Jesus said. They couldn't understand it when He said, "I am come down from heaven." They whispered among themselves asking each other, "Is not this Jesus, the son of Joseph, whose father and mother we know? How is it then that He saith, I came down from heaven?"

Jesus therefore answered and said unto them, "Murmur not among yourselves. No man can come to me, except the Father which hath sent me draw him: and I will raise him up at the last day. It is written in the prophets, and they shall be all taught of God. Every man therefore that hath heard, and hath learned of the Father, cometh unto me. Not that any man hath seen the Father, except he which is of God, he hath seen the Father.

"What shall we do that we might work the works of God? Our fathers did eat manna in the desert," Jesus said. "As it is written, he gave them bread from heaven to eat. Verily, verily, I say unto you, Moses gave you not that bread from heaven, but my Father gives you the true bread from heaven. For, the bread of God is He which came down from heaven to give life unto the world."

And, they pleaded with him, saying, "Lord, give us this bread."

Jesus, then, made all things clear to the multitude by saying, "I am the bread which came down from heaven to give life unto the world."

Still, the multitude did not understand for they implored Jesus, "Lord, give us this bread!"

How is it then that he saith, I came down from heaven?"

Jesus therefore answered and said unto them, "Murmur

71

not among your selves. No man can come to me, except the Father which hath sent me draw him: and I will raise him up at the last day. It is written in the prophets, and they shall be all taught of God. Every man therefore that hath heard, and hath learned of the Father, cometh unto me. Not that any man hath seen the Father, except He which is of God, He hath seen the Father.

"Verily, verily, I say unto you, He that believeth on me hath everlasting life." Again, Jesus declares, "I am that bread of life. Your fathers did eat manna in the wilderness, and are dead. This is the bread which cometh down from heaven, that a man may eat thereof, and not die. I am the living bread which came down from heaven: if any man eats of this bread, he shall live forever: and the bread that I will give is my flesh, which I will give for the life of the world."

Jesus, in the aforementioned verses of scripture, openly stated that He is the Son of God, and that what He was doing was God's will whatever they ate and whatever they drank was only sustenance to keep them alive. But, He declared, if they believe in Him and take Him into their lives, He, being the "true bread" of life, will ultimately give them life everlasting. He told them that "everyone that sees the Son, and believes in Him, will have everlasting life" because He will raise them up on the last day; that is to say, the day of judgment.

"The Jews therefore strove among themselves, saying, "How can this man give us *his* flesh to eat?" They still didn't fully understand.

Jesus spoke again, saying, "Except ye eat the flesh of the Son of Man, and drink His blood, ye have no life in you. Whoever eats my flesh, and drinks my blood, will have eternal life; and I will raise him up at the last day. My flesh is meat indeed, and my blood is drink indeed. He that eats my flesh, and drinks my blood, dwells in me, and I in him.

"As the living Father hath sent me, and I live by the Father: so he that eats of me, even he shall live by me. This is that bread which came down from heaven: not as your fathers did eat manna, and are dead: he that eats of this bread shall live forever."

Jesus spoke these words in the synagogue as He taught in Capernaum.

Many of His disciples, when they had heard *this*, said, "What is He talking about? Those who hear Him will not tolerate what He is teaching?"

Jesus knew what was on many of His disciple's minds. And, He asked them, "Does what I say offend you?" Jesus, the gospel tells us, knew from the beginning which disciples did not believe Him, and who would betray Him.

From this time on, many of Jesus' disciples left Him and walked no more with Him. And Jesus asked the twelve, "Will ye also leave me?"

To this, Simon Peter said, "Lord, to whom shall we go? We know that you have the words to eternal life." And, Peter breathed deeply and added, "We believe, and are sure, that thou art the Christ, the Son of the living God."

Jesus said, "Have I not chosen you twelve, and one of you is a devil?" Jesus was speaking of Judas Iscariot; the son of Simon, for he it was that should betray Him, being one of the twelve.

*****

Note: If you believe that Christ is the Son of the living God, as did Peter, and truly want to serve Christ, get in touch with us via email. You need not question "Lord, to whom shall we go?" We will prepare you to do God's work here on Earth as a doctor in our Church if this is what you truly want to do. Email us at cguerra@hvc.rr.com.

*****

The Holy Bible

*****

Chapter VIII

Jesus Tells His Disciples to Always be ready
Jesus Teaches In the Temple
The Mount of Olives

After this, Jesus went straight away into Galilee. And, even though the Jews' Feast of Tabernacles was at hand, He decided not to go for He was well aware that the Jews sought to kill him. He knew that his time had not yet come.

*****

Before going on, I would like to enlighten those of you who do not know exactly what the Feast of Tabernacles is and why it is important to the Jews. I have researched this holiday and have found that Wikipedia, the internet Free Encyclopaedia, explains it best.

Another name for Feast of Tabernacles would be Sukkot, meaning *"place"* in Hebrew (though it also has other meanings). It is, of course, a Jewish Biblical Holiday celebrated on the 15th day of the month of Tishrei (late September to late October). It is one of the three biblically mandated Shalosh regalim on which Jews and Believers make pilgrimages to pre-determined sites to worship and make fellowship in the Temple in Jerusalem.

The Holy Week lasts seven days, including Chol Hammed and is immediately followed by another festive day known as Shemini Atzeret. The Hebrew word *sukkot* is the plural of *sukkah*, "booth or tabernacle", which is a walled structure covered with flora, such as tree branches or bamboo shoots.

The sukkah is intended as a reminiscence of the type of fragile dwellings in which the ancient Israelites dwelt during their 40 years of wandering in the desert after the Exodus from Egypt.

Throughout the holiday the sukkah becomes the

primary living area of one's home. All meals are eaten inside the sukkah and many sleep there as well. On each day of the holiday, members of the household recite a blessing over the <u>lulav</u> and <u>Etrog</u>, or <u>four species</u>.[1]According to <u>Zechariah</u>, in the <u>messianic era</u> Sukkot will become a universal festival and all nations will make pilgrimages annually to <u>Jerusalem</u> to celebrate the feast there.[2]

Sukkot became one of the most important feasts in Judaism, as indicated by its designation as "the Feast of the Lord" [5] or simply "the Feast".[6] Perhaps because of its wide attendance, Sukkot became the appropriate time for important state ceremonies.[7] <u>Moses</u> instructed the children of Israel to gather for a reading of the Law during Sukkot every seventh year (Deut. 31:10-11). <u>King Solomon</u> dedicated the <u>Temple in Jerusalem</u> on Sukkot (1 Kings 8; 2 Chron. 7). And Sukkot was the first sacred occasion observed after the resumption of sacrifices in Jerusalem following the <u>Babylonian captivity</u> (Ezra 3:2-4). In <u>Leviticus</u>, God told Moses to command the people: "On the first day you shall take the product of hadar trees, branches of palm trees, boughs of leafy trees, and <u>willows</u> of the brook" (Lev. 23:40), and "You shall live in booths seven days; all citizens in Israel shall live in booths, in order that future generations may know that I made the Israelite people live in booths when I brought them out of the land of <u>Egypt</u>" (Lev. 23:42-43). Sukkot is a seven day holiday, with the first day celebrated as a full festival with special prayer services and holiday meals. The remaining days are known as <u>Chol HaMoed</u> ("festival weekdays"). The seventh day of Sukkot is called <u>Hoshana Rabbah</u> ("Great Hoshana", referring to the tradition that worshippers in the <u>synagogue</u> walk around the perimeter of the sanctuary during morning services) and has a special observance of its own. Outside Israel, the first two days are celebrated as full festivals. Throughout the week of Sukkot, meals are eaten in the sukkah and some families sleep there, although the requirement is waived in case of rain. Chabad Hassidim do not sleep in the sukkah even in good weather [8]. Every day, a blessing is recited over the Lulav and the Etrog. Observance of Sukkot is detailed in the Book of Nehemiah in the Bible, the Mishnah (Sukkah 1:1–5:8); the Tosefta (Sukkah 1:1–4:28); and the Jerusalem Talmud (Sukkah 1a–) and Babylonian Talmud (Sukkah 2a–56b).

You can learn more about this Biblical Holiday by going to: http://en.wikipedia.org/wiki/Sukkot

*****

So, Jesus said to his disciples, "My time is not yet come, but you must be always ready. The world cannot hate you; but me it hates because I testify of it, that the works thereof are evil." He paused a few seconds and then continued, "Go ye up unto the feast without me. For, I cannot go yet because my time is not yet full come." After He had said this, His disciples left Him and He remained in Galilee for a little while.

But when His brethren were gone up, then went He also up unto the feast, not openly, but as it were in secret. But, when Jesus was there, we are informed by John that the Jews were looking for Him, asking the people, "Where is he?"

Surely the order was given to find Jesus because the last time He was there He healed a man on the Sabbath. The mere fact that they were seeking Him had to mean that they wanted to arrest Him.

There was a lot of murmuring among those at the feast. Some were saying good things about Him while others were offended by Him. Many of those at the feast were told that Jesus was deceiving them. These rumors, of course, were started by the Jews who were in control of the temple. No man spoke openly of Jesus in the temple because they were afraid.

But, Jesus went up in the midst of the gatherings and taught openly. And those that heard Him marveled, saying, "How knoweth this man letters, having never learned?"

Jesus replied, "My doctrine is not mine, but His that sent me. If any man will do His will, he shall know of the doctrine, whether it is of God, or whether I speak of myself. He that speaks of himself seeks his own glory, but he that seeks the glory of Him that sent him, the same is true, and there is no unrighteousness in him."

Jesus paused, then continued, "Wasn't it Moses who gave you the law and yet none of you keep it? So why do you go about looking to kill me?"

One of the Jews said, "What are you talking about? Who is looking to kill you? Thou hast a devil!"

Then cried Jesus in the temple as He taught, saying, "Ye both know me, and ye know whence I am: and I am not come of myself, but He that sent me is true, whom ye know not. But I know Him: for I am from Him, and He hath sent me."

The Jews wanted to take Him but no man laid a hand on Him because His time had not yet come. Many of the people believed in Jesus and whispered to each other, "When Christ comes; He will be able to do more miracles than these which this man has done?"

By this statement, we can only assume that the people were impressed with Jesus because of the miracles He had done. Surely, it is safe to say that many were offended by what He said but, because of the miracles He did, they leaned towards believing that He was the Christ (Messiah).

By the statement, "When Christ comes," is to imply or infer that He's not here yet. But, "When Christ comes," will Christ (the true Christ) be able to do, not what Jesus has done, but *more* than the miracles that this man has done?" There can be no argument that Jesus impressed the multitudes by performing miracles more so than by what He said. At least up until this point.

Up until now, it is safe to assume that, even though Jesus had compassion for the blind, the lame, the deaf, and all others who were diseased, He healed them primarily to prove His divinity. Who but the Son of God could cause a man to see who was born blind? Who but God could bring a dead man back to life? By Jesus' acts of mercy in doing these things, it is safe to say that these things helped him to lay the foundation of His divinity for the purpose of what was to bring about the culmination of His mission here on earth. Let us continue.

The Pharisees heard the people talking of Jesus and of the miracles He had done, and of the things He was teaching, and sought to take Him. Then said Jesus unto them, "Yet a little while am I with you, and *then* I go unto him that sent me. Ye shall seek me, and shall not find *me:* and where I am, *thither* ye cannot come."

Then said the Jews among themselves, "Where will he go that we shall not find him? Will he go unto the dispersed among the Gentiles, and teach the Gentiles?"

Others said, "What *manner of* saying is this that he said, 'Ye shall seek me, and shall not find *me:* and where I am, *thither* ye cannot come?'"They just did not understand what Jesus was saying.

They could not lay hold of Jesus simply because His time had not come for the prophecies to be fulfilled. He was able to continue in the temple all during the Feast of the Tabernacles. And on the last day, Jesus stood and cried out, "If any man thirst let him come unto me, and drink. He that believeth on me, as the scripture hath said, out of his belly shall flow rivers of living water." But this spake He of the Holy Ghost which they that believe on Him should receive: for the Holy Ghost was not yet *given;* because that Jesus was not yet glorified.

Many who had heard Jesus say these words were convinced, saying, "Of a truth, this is the Prophet!" Others said, "This is the Christ!" Still, others said, "Shall Christ come out of Galilee?"

Does not the scripture say that Christ will be of the seed of David and out of the town of Bethlehem where David was? These questions all arose among the people and they were divided concerning Jesus and what they thought of him.

The Chief Priests and the Pharisees, then, said to the officers, "Why haven't you brought Him?"

The officers replied, "Never has any man spoken like this man."

Angrily, the Pharisees said, "Are you also deceived?"

Have any of the rulers or the Pharisees believed in Him? But the people who did not know the law were cursed. Nicodemus was also among them while this was going on. He remembered how he went to Jesus by night and the things Jesus said to him. Nicodemus, in truth, was indeed one of Jesus' followers because he believed in Jesus.

Nicodemus spoke out, "Does our law judge any man before it hears him and what it is he is doing?"

The Chief Priests and Pharisees responded, "Are you

also of Galilee? Search and look: for out of Galilee ariseth *no* prophet!"

*****

And each man went his own way as Jesus went unto the Mount of Olives.

The Mount of Olives (also Mount Olivet, <u>Hebrew</u>: הר הזיתים, *Har HaZeitim* ;<u>Arabic</u>: جبل الزيتون، الطور, *Jebel az-Zeitun*) is a mountain ridge in eastern <u>Jerusalem</u> with three peaks running from north to south.[1] The highest, at-Tur, rises to 818 meters (2,683 ft.).[2] It is named for the <u>olive groves</u> that once covered its slopes. The Mount of Olives is associated predominantly with <u>Jewish</u> and <u>Christian</u> traditions but also contains several sites important in <u>Islam</u>. The mount has been used as a Jewish cemetery for over 3,000 years and holds approximately 150,000 graves.

From Biblical times until today, Jews have been buried on the Mount of Olives. The <u>necropolis on the southern ridge</u>, the location of the modern village of <u>Silwan</u>, was the burial place of the city's most important citizens in the period of the Biblical kings.[4] There are an estimated 150,000 graves on the Mount, including tombs traditionally associated with <u>Zechariah</u> and <u>Avshalom</u>. On the upper slope, the traditional <u>Tomb of the Prophets Haggai, Zechariah and Malachi</u> is situated. Notable rabbis buried on the mount include <u>Chaim ibn Attar</u> and others from the 15th-century to present.

<u>Roman soldiers</u> from the <u>10th Legion</u> camped on the Mount during the <u>Siege of Jerusalem</u> in the year 70 CE. The religious ceremony marking the start of a new month was held on the Mount of Olives in the days of the <u>Second Temple</u>.[5] After the destruction of the Temple, Jews celebrated the festival of <u>Sukkot</u> on the Mount of Olives.

They made pilgrimages to the Mount of Olives because it was 80 meters higher than the Temple Mount and offered a panoramic view of the Temple site. It became a traditional place for lamenting the Temple's destruction, especially on Tisha B'Av.

In 1481, an Italian Jewish pilgrim, Rabbi Meshulam Da Volterra, wrote: "And all the community of Jews, every year, goes up to Mount Zion on the day of Tisha B'Av to fast and mourn, and from there they move down along Yoshafat Valley and up to Mount of Olives. From there they see the whole Temple (the Temple Mount) and there they weep and lament the destruction of this House." (The Temple)

In the mid-1850s, the villagers of Silwan were paid £100 annually by the Jews in an effort to prevent the desecration of graves on the mount. During the Islamization of Jerusalem under Jordanian occupation from 1948 to 1967, Jewish burials were halted, massive vandalism took place, and 40,000 of the 50,000 graves were desecrated. King Hussein permitted the construction of the Intercontinental Hotel at the summit of the Mount of Olives together with a road that cut through the cemetery which destroyed hundreds of Jewish graves, some from the First Temple Period. After the Six-Day War, restoration work began, and the cemetery was re-opened for burials.

Israeli Prime Minister, Menachem Begin asked to be buried on the Mount of Olives near the grave of Etzel member Meir Feinstein, rather than Mount Herzl national cemetery. (All information above courtesy of http://en.wikipedia.org)

Jesus spent the night on the Mount of Olives in prayer. In the morning, He returned to the temple and began to teach. As He was teaching, the scribes and Pharisees came to Him dragging a woman who had been taken, they said, in the very act of adultery and set her in the midst where Jesus was teaching.

One of the Pharisees said to Jesus, "Master, this woman had been taken in adultery; in the very act. Now Moses in the law commanded us, that such should be stoned: <u>Lev. 20.10</u> · <u>Deut. 22.22-24</u> but what sayest thou?" Of course, they were tempting Jesus because they wanted to be able to charge Him with not adhering to the Law of Moses.

The Law of Moses directed that the woman *should* be stoned. So, if Jesus said, "don't stone her," or anything else contrary to the Law, He would be guilty of blasphemy and would be arrested.

But, Jesus knew why the scribes and Pharisees were there and would not be deceived. Jesus, then, stooped down and with His finger, wrote something on the ground as though He wasn't even listening to them. So, when they continued to ask Jesus, "what sayest thou?" He stood and said, "Let he among you who is without sin cast the first stone." Again, He stooped down and wrote on the ground. And they which heard *it,* being convicted by *their own* conscience, went out one by one, beginning at the eldest, *even* unto the last: and Jesus was left alone, and the woman standing in the midst.

When Jesus stood up and saw no one standing there, He asked the woman, "Woman, where are your accusers? Hath no man condemned you?"

"No man, Lord," the woman said.

And Jesus replied, "Neither do I condemn thee. Go and sin no more."

Many have speculated as to what Jesus had written on the ground. No one can be sure what Jesus had written or, indeed, if He wrote anything at all! Those who assumed

Jesus wrote something on the ground were only guessing. Perhaps He sought to intimidate those who had accused the woman of adultery by writing the sins of the woman's accusers so they would know Jesus knew that they were not sinless. No one knows what was written, if anything.

Nevertheless, even though Jesus was well aware of Mosaic Law dictating that the woman was to be stoned to death, He demonstrated, here, a compassion and willingness to offer forgiveness, and mercy, when, had they not approached Jesus, there would have been none.

The only reason the scribes and Pharisees brought the woman to Jesus was to attempt to "trap" Him into breaking the law. In truth, it doesn't matter at all whether or not Jesus wrote on the ground. Whatever many might have guessed that He wrote, the point is; that which I receive from this event, is that Christ is Savior and through Him, alone, are our sins forgiven.

Jesus knew that the woman's accusers were not without sin and He shamed them by stating, "Let he who is without sin cast the first stone." Jesus could very well have pointed out their sins to the crowd of people present. The scribes and Pharisees knew this. So, one by one, those ready to throw stones dropped them and slowly left. Jesus is the only one who is sinless and He said, "Woman, where are your accusers? Hath no man condemned you?"

"No," the woman replied.

The only one who could have condemned the woman did not. Jesus, then, demonstrating love, forgiveness, and mercy, told the woman, "Neither do I condemn thee." Then, He instructed her, "Go and sin no more."

So, once again, the Jews were not able to "trap" Jesus into breaking the Laws of Moses. The reason they failed was because "his time had not yet come."

I must pause here to talk about the beheading of John the Baptist. Because the purpose of this book is to focus on Jesus, I will say little about John's death since St. John's Gospel gives no details and description of this event as indicated below:

In the Gospels account of John's death, Herod has John imprisoned for denouncing his marriage, and John is later executed by beheading.

John condemned Herod for marrying <u>Herodias</u>, the former wife of his brother Philip, in violation of Old Testament Law. Later Herodias' daughter <u>Salome</u> dances before Herod, who offers her a favor in return. Herodias tells her to ask for the head of John the Baptist, which is delivered to her on a plate (Mark 6:14-29).

The first century Jewish historian Josephus gives a slightly different account in his *Antiquities of the Jews.* Josephus writes that Herod had John arrested because John had so many followers that Herod feared they might begin a rebellion. Herod later had him executed (*Ant.* 18.116-118). It is possible that both accounts are true. Josephus writes about John's death in a section detailing some of Herod's political dealings. Herod regarded John as a threat. He spoke against Herod and had many followers, so Herod wanted to get rid of him. The Gospels recall the teaching of John, that he called for Israel to purify herself through baptism (Matthew 3:1-12). So the Gospels' description of John's death focuses on the final reason Herod had for arresting John, which was religious. So it may have been that Herod wanted John arrested because he was a political threat, and John's condemnations of Herod's marriage was "the final straw". See James D.G. Dunn, *Jesus) A (This information courtesy of: Rememhttp://en.wikipedia.org/wiki/John_the_Baptistbered* pp377–379.

*****

"For God so loved the world He gave His only begotten Son that whosoever believeth in Him should not perish but have everlasting life." John 3:16

★★★★★

Chapter IX

The Pharisees Challenge Jesus
Jesus Heals the Man Blind from Birth

A multitude of people soon gathered about   Jesus, again, while He was in the treasury. And He said, "I am the light of the world; he that follows me shall not walk in darkness but shall have the light of life."

A Pharisee interrupted and said, "You are talking about yourself. What you are saying is not true!"

Jesus turned to the Pharisee and replied, "Though I bear record of myself, my record *is* true. I know whence I came, and hither I go. But *ye* cannot tell from whence I came or whither I go." He paused, and then continued, "You judge after the flesh; I judge no man. But," he added, "if I do judge, my judgment is true: For I am not alone because the Father who sent me is with me.

"It is also written in your law," Jesus said, "that the testimony of two men bears truth. I am one that bears witness of myself, as does the Father who sent me. He also bears witness of me."

The Pharisees asked him, "Where is thy father?"

Jesus answered, "You neither know me, nor do you know my Father. If you had known me, you would know my Father."

And, again, no one laid a hand on Him because His time had not yet come. Jesus had spoken some powerful words that surely angered the scribes and Pharisees who heard. Yet, Jesus' hour had not come for He had much more to do and say to those who sought after Him.

Jesus spoke out again, saying "I go my way, and you shall seek me, and die in your sins. Where I am going; you cannot come."

The Jews thought to themselves, "Why does he say that where he goes we cannot come? Is he going to kill himself?"

"You are from beneath" Jesus said. "I am from above. You are of this world; I am not of this world." Jesus continued, "I said that you shall die in your sins, for if you don't believe that I am he, you shall die in your sins."

"Who are you?" the Jews asked, again.

"I have told you who I was from the beginning." Jesus paused, and then added, "I have many things to say and to judge of you; but he that sent me is true, and I speak to the world of the things I have heard of him."

The Jews just didn't understand that He was speaking to them about the Father.

Jesus said unto them, "When you have lifted up the Son of Man, then will you know that I am he, and that I do nothing of myself, but as my Father had taught me, I speak these things.

"And he that sent me is with me; the Father has not left me alone; for I do always the things that please him."

As Jesus spoke these words, many who heard him speak believed.

And Jesus spoke directly to those whom He knew believed. He said, "If you continue in my word, than you are my disciples, indeed. You shall know the truth, and the truth shall set you free."

The Jews answered him, saying, "We are of Abraham's seed and were never in bondage to any man. Why do you say, you shall be made free?"

We must stop here because the Jews, in responding to Jesus, when they stated, "We are of Abraham's seed and were never in bondage," was a false statement. Wasn't the seed of Abraham in bondage to the Egyptians? Were they not often in bondage to the neighboring nations, in the time of the Judges? Weren't they captives for 70 years in Babylon? Was they not, at this time tributaries to the Romans, and though not in a personal, yet in a national bondage to them? And yet, to confront Christ, they have the impudence to say, "We were never in bondage!" This, of course, was a foolish assertion and not even argumentative.

Were the Jews inferring that they, as individuals, were not slaves; one man having one master? The implication was ridiculous and should not have been made.

In verse 37, Jesus replies, "I know that ye are Abraham's seed; but ye seek to kill me, because my word hath no place in you." He continues, "I speak that which I have seen with my Father: and ye do that which ye have seen with your father."

"Abraham is our father!" they cried out.

"If you were Abraham's children, you would do the works of Abraham. Instead, you are looking to kill me even though I tell you the truth. You do the deeds of *your* father."

The Jews cried out, "We are not born of fornication! We have one Father who is God!"

"If God was your Father, you would love me," Jesus said. "I came from God; it is he who has sent me." He paused, and then continued, "You come from your father, the devil! He was a murderer from the beginning! He didn't tell the truth because there was no truth in him. When he speaks, he speaks only lies because he is the father of lies! And, though I tell you the truth, you don't believe me. I speak that which I have seen with my Father: and you do that which you have seen with *your* father."

The Jews responded angrily, "You must be a Samaritan! You have a devil!"

"I have no devil!" Jesus exclaimed. "I am honoring my Father and you dishonor me! I seek not glory for myself but He who seeks and judges! I tell you this: if a man keeps my sayings, he shall never see death!"

"Now we know that you have a devil," they said. "Abraham and the prophets are all dead and you still say that if a man keeps your sayings he will never taste of death! Are you greater than our father Abraham, and the prophets who are all dead? Who do you think you are?"

Appearing almost frustrated, Jesus said, "If I bring honor to myself, it means nothing! It is my Father who honors me; he whom you refer to as your God! Yet you've never known him. But, I know him. And if I say I don't know him, I am a liar. But, I know him and keep his sayings."

Jesus sighed and then spoke, "Your father, Abraham, rejoiced to see my day, and he saw it, and was glad."

"You are not yet fifty years old and you stand there and tell us you've seen Abraham?"

"Before Abraham was," Jesus replied, "I was."

The Jews, than, not understanding, picked up stones to stone Him. But, Jesus escaped by hiding himself. Soon, thereafter, He left the temple.

*****

Later, Jesus saw a man who was blind from birth. And, his disciples asked Him, "Master, who did sin; this man or his parents that he was born blind?"

Jesus explained, saying, "Neither has this man sinned or his parents; but that the works of God should be made manifest in him." Simply put, the Jews believed that a deformity of some kind, or any kind of a birth defect was the effect of sin of either the parents or another descendant.

Jesus made it very clear that such was not the case. Jesus came upon the blind man and was to demonstrate the miraculous power of God to the world.

Jesus, unlike the rulers and priests of the temple was to show all of us that mercy and compassion is needed. We are not to cast blame and distance ourselves from a traditional opinion that this man, or any other person, should be shamed because his or her condition was brought about by the sin of another. Jesus' action in the case of this man who was born blind is an example of mercy and love that all of us should follow every minute of our lives.

In this case of the man who was born blind, we see the wise and wonderful arrangement of Divine Providence. It is a part of His great plan to adapt His mercies to the woes of men: and often calamity, want, poverty, and sickness are permitted, that He may show the provisions of His mercy; that He may teach us to prize his blessings, and that deep-felt gratitude for deliverance may bind us to Him. (*This paragraph taken from http://bible.cc/John/9-3.htm*)

After Jesus had spoken, He spat on the ground and made clay of the spittle and anointed the blind man's eyes with the clay.

A question now arises which has been bothering many people for a lot of years. Why did Jesus use clay to heal the blind man? Of course, Jesus could have just said the word and the blind man would have been healed. Instead, the Gospel of John tells us that Jesus spat on the ground and made clay of the dust and rubbed it on the man's eyes. Why? What could have been the reason for doing this?

In truth, no one really knows the answer to this question although many have speculated as to why. The mere fact that man was made by God from the dust of the ground, as indicated in the Book of Genesis could have been a reason. In other words, the man being born without sight was here and now being made right by God. Another guess would be that to "heal" a person using mud during this period of time was, in fact, against the law; Jesus might have used this method to irritate and annoy the rulers and priests. But, in essence, nobody really knows why Jesus didn't just say the word to restore the man's sight.

Above all else, Jesus' healing of the man who was born blind and made "available" to Jesus at the time was because, as Jesus said, was "that the works of God should be made manifest in him." Simply put, without guess work or speculation, the man was there for Christ to heal as a demonstration of God's power. The Lord made it clear that someone's prior sin had nothing to do with the man's physical condition. And, He, by healing the blind man, made it clear that all nonsense aside, <u>God is loving and merciful</u>.

"Go and wash in the pool of Siloam," Jesus instructed. The man went as instructed, washed his eyes, and was able to see.

When those who witnessed the event saw what Jesus had done and saw the man was able to see they were amazed. Many who had witnessed the event mumbled amongst themselves asking, "Is not this he who has sat and begged?"

Others remarked, "He is like him!"

And the man who was blind whom Jesus had healed replied, "I am he."

Those that were there asked him, "How were your eyes opened?"

"A man called Jesus made clay and anointed my eyes, and told me to go in the Pool of Siloam and wash. I did as He instructed, and I am now able to see."

Looking about, they that were there asked the man,

"Where is He?"

"I don't know!" the man cried.

Some of the Jews, then, took the once blind man to the Pharisees. Be reminded that this was the Sabbath Day that Jesus made the clay and anointed the man's eyes.

The Pharisees, themselves, asked the once blind man how he had received his sight.

And, the man repeated, saying, "He put clay on my eyes and told me to wash them. I did as He instructed and now I can see!"

The Pharisees said, "This is no man of God because He does not keep the Sabbath."

Others said, "How can such a man be a sinner when He does such miracles?"

One of the Jews said, "What have you to say of the man who opened your eyes?"

The man who was once blind replied, speaking slowly, "He is a prophet."

Many of the Jews, and the Pharisees, did not believe that the man was born blind, or, was ever blind. So, they summoned the man's parents, and asked them, "Is this your son? Was he born blind? If he was, tell us how it is that he can now see!"

The parents replied, "This is our son. And, he was born without sight. But, by what means he now sees, we know not; or who has opened his eyes. He is of age; ask him. He can speak for himself."

The Pharisees, then, called the man who was once blind, again, and said to him, "Give God the praise. We know that this man is a sinner (meaning, Jesus)."

The man who was blind responded, "Whether He is a sinner or not; I don't know. One thing I do know is, I was blind, and now I see."

Angrily, the Pharisees scolded the man, saying, "You are His disciple. We are Moses' disciple!" They continued, "We know that God spoke to Moses. But, we don't know where this man comes from!"

The man replied, solemnly, "Why, this is a marvelous thing. You say you know not from whence He is but this man has opened my eyes." The man hesitated a few seconds and then continued, "We know that God doesn't hear sinners but He does hear those who worship Him. If this man were not from God He could do nothing."

The Jews replied, "You were born in sin and dare to teach us?" They, then, cast the man out from amongst them.

Word got back to Jesus that the Jews cast the man out, and when he found the man, he asked him, "Do you believe in the Son of God?"

"Who is He, Lord that I might believe in Him?" the man asked.

"You have seen Him, and it is He that talks to you."

The man said, "Lord, I believe." He, then, fell down and worshipped Jesus.

And Jesus said, "For judgment I am come into this world, that they which see not might see; and that they which see might be made blind."

Some of the Pharisees who heard Jesus, asked Him, "Are we blind, also?"

Jesus said unto them," If ye were blind, you should have no sin: ut now you say, we see; therefore your sin remains."

*****

The story of the man born blind is certainly recorded for all to read for a couple of good reasons. The first reason, of course, demonstrates the tremendous power of Almighty God. The man was born blind and still Jesus was able to give sight to him.

Also, there is no indication that the man *had* eyes or that he *didn't* have eyes. The Gospel of John does not mention this point. The mere fact that Jesus made the clay and rubbed the man's eyes could have been an indication that the man *had* no eyes, just empty sockets. Christ did not just restore sight to a blind man; He gave him sight <u>*he never had*</u>. Those present witnessed the tremendous power of God.

The event concerning the man born blind should also make every one of us aware of another very important point that Jesus emphasized. The very words of Jesus when asked by the Pharisees, "are we blind, also?"

Jesus replied very quickly. He said, ".... You say you see, therefore your sin remains."

If you tell others you're a Christian, and teach Sunday school, and do all you can to help the church, it doesn't matter if you don't conduct yourself as a Christian every day of the week. We can quote Bible verses and even be a deacon of the church. But, if we do not let God take control of our lives we, as the bible says, become as sounding brass. We become like the Pharisees who said they loved God but had neither charity, or love for those who worshipped in the temple.

*****

Chapter X
Jesus Describes Himself as the Good Shepherd
Jesus Is God!
The Holy Trinity
Jesus Raises Lazarus

Jesus, then, talks about the sheepfold and the door. He makes it clear that He is the door and the sheepfold is the Church. He is telling the world that all who enter the Church must enter by the door. Jesus speaks saying, "I am the door and if any man enters in, he shall be saved."

Jesus now distinguishes Himself from those who came before Him. He says, "Those who came before me were thieves and robbers." He tells them that they, the sheep, did not follow them because they did not recognize them as they should. He made it clear that those who came before Him came to steal, and kill, and to destroy. Jesus tells them, "I have come so that the sheep of my flock might have life, and that they might have it more abundantly.

"I am the Good Shepherd," Jesus tells them. "The Good Shepherd gives His life for the sheep. He who is hired goes away because they are not his sheep. He doesn't care what happens to them. And, I have other sheep that are not of this fold. They also hear my voice. Soon there will be one fold and one Shepherd."

Jesus looked directly into the eyes of those He knew were against Him. He said, "No man will take my life from me. I lay it down myself. I have the power to lay my life down and then to live again. I have received this power from my Father in heaven."

After Jesus spoke these words, many of those who heard Him cried out angrily, saying, "This man is mad! Why do you listen to Him! He has a devil!"

Others defended Jesus saying, "These are not the words

of a man who has a devil! Can a devil open the eyes of the blind?"

Jesus turned and left and later walked in Solomon's porch. The Gospel of John reminds us that it was winter. But the Jews followed Jesus and formed a circle around Him. They shouted out, "If you be the Christ (Messiah), tell us plainly!"

Jesus answered them," I told you, and you believed not: the works that I do in my Father's name, they bear witness of me. But you believe not, because you are not of my sheep, as I said unto you."

Jesus added, calmly, "My sheep hear my voice and they know me. I know them and they follow me. I give my sheep eternal life; they shall never perish. And no one will be able to pluck them out of my hand." Jesus continued, "My Father who gave them to me is the greatest of all. No one is able to pluck them out of my Father's hand." Jesus sighed and then added, "I and my Father are one."

When Jesus said this, those that heard Him were furious because they misunderstood what He was saying. They interpreted what Jesus said to mean "He is God." Jesus never said He was God. Jesus was referring to His mission; His purpose for being on earth. And, because they didn't understand what Jesus meant when He said, "I and my Father are one," they became furious and began picking up stones to kill Him. For Jesus to say that He was God would be blasphemy and, surely, they would want to kill Him on the spot.

Remember, also, that at that time, Jesus had not yet risen from the dead, and the Church, of course, had not yet been established. Jesus had a mission and until that mission was accomplished and the Church was established, only a minute number of followers barely were beginning to understand just exactly who Jesus was, what His purpose for being on earth was, and exactly what His status concerning His divinity was, then, now, today, and forever.

Most Christian Churches teach what is referred to as the Holy Trinity. I believe, as do most Christians, that there are three entities that make up the Holy Trinity. This, to me, means that there are three entities that make up the God Head. They are, God, the Father, Jesus Christ, the Son, and the Comforter/Holy Ghost.

Jesus Christ, to many Christians is God incarnate. This means, simply, that Jesus is God who became man to carry out an earthly mission to bring salvation to all mankind. Now, does this mean that God and Jesus Christ are one and the same? No one can be sure because, as we are not gods ourselves, or even demigods, it could be that we lack the intelligence, or wisdom to make such a determination.

Could it be that Jehovah God, Jesus Christ, and the Holy Ghost, are three separate entities who are identified as God who should, or could be, identified as "Gods"? This *could* be the case. The Gospel according to St. John says, "In the beginning was the Word, and the Word was with God, and the Word was God." Let's examine these words carefully. In the beginning was the Word. The word, Word, being capitalized obviously refers to a person, or entity. The Word; that is to say, this person or entity was with God. So, someone was with God. And, the Word; this someone <u>was</u> God! What we are being told is that someone who was God was, Himself, God. In essence, we are being told that in the beginning was a God who was with another God. This, of course, is the inference most reasonable or educated people would surmise.

We than read, "All things were made by him..." The Gospel writer is telling us that this "other" God made all

98

things (referring to the creation) and without Him was not anything made that was made." This "other" God, as He is described, is the "light" of the world.

Verse 14 of John's Gospel tells us, "And the Word was made flesh, and dwelt among us (and we beheld his glory, the glory as of the only begotten of the Father), full of grace and truth." John is telling us that the Word, who was with God, and who was God, was made flesh and dwelt among us. The Word, God; John makes clear is the only begotten of the Father and is full of grace and truth. John, of course, is referring to Jesus Christ, in that He, being the Word, or the other God, was born into the world and being flesh, as other men, lived in the world as one filled with grace and truth.

It is easy, now, based on the scriptures, to understand the fact that Jehovah God and Jesus Christ *is* God. Both are God, and yet both are individual persons. But, even as the Jews did not understand Jesus when He told them, "I and my Father are one," so it might be difficult for some to comprehend the fact that; even though Jehovah God and Jesus Christ are both God, together, they are one God.

"But, (you may ask if you do not know already) how can this be?" It is not that difficult to understand if you believe the scriptures and the teachings of the Church. But, first, let us examine how the Comforter, or Holy Spirit, fits into this picture.

As scripture was inspired and man began to write the word, it was evident to the writers that God was made of more than One Person later to be defined as the "Triune God." Although the word triune is not mentioned in the Bible, we know that there are three very distinct Persons that make up the Godhead. They are all equal in every way. They are Omnipotent-All powerful. Luke 1:35, "And the angel answered and said unto her, 'The Holy Spirit shall come upon you, and the power of the Highest shall overshadow you: therefore also that holy thing which shall be born of you shall be called the Son of God.'"

They are Omnipresent - at all places at once. Psalms 139:7-10, "Where shall I go from your Spirit? Or where shall I flee from your presence? "If I ascend up into heaven, thou art there: if I make my bed in hell, behold, thou art there; If I take the wings of the morning, and dwell in the uttermost parts of the sea; even there shall thy hand lead me, and thy right hand shall hold me."

They are Omniscient - All knowing. 1 Corinthians 2:10, "But God has revealed them unto us by his Spirit: for the Spirit searches all things, yea the deep things of God." And, these three persons of the Godhead are eternal and equal.

Read the Book of Hebrews 9:14. It tells us, "How much more shall the blood of Christ, who through the eternal Spirit offered himself without spot to God, purge your conscience from dead works to serve the living God?" And, also, the Book of Acts 5:3-4 where we read, "But Peter said, Ananias, why has Satan filled your heart to lie to the Holy Spirit, and to keep back part of the price of the land? While it remained, was it not your own? And after it was sold, was it not in your own power? Why have you conceived this thing in your heart? You have not lied unto men, but unto God."

There are many scriptural references that prove the co-existence of the entities, or Persons, that make up the Holy Trinity, or Godhead. Luke 3:22, "And the Holy Ghost descended in a bodily shape like a dove upon Him, and a voice came from heaven, which said, "Thou art my beloved Son; in thee I am well pleased." Here we see the evidence of the Father, Son, and Holy Spirit all mentioned within one verse.

We also see the same reference elsewhere in the Gospels. Matthew 3:16-17, "And Jesus, when he was baptized, went up straightway out of the water: and, lo, the heavens were opened unto him, and he saw the Spirit of God descending like a dove, and lighting upon him: And lo a voice from heaven, saying, this is my beloved Son, in whom I am well pleased."

Mark 1:10-13, "And straightway coming up out of the water, He saw the heavens opened, and the Spirit like a dove descending upon Him: And there came a voice from heaven, saying, Thou art my beloved Son, in whom I am well pleased. And immediately the Spirit driveth Him into the wilderness. And He was there in the wilderness forty days, tempted of Satan; and was with the wild beasts; and the angels ministered unto Him."

Deuteronomy demonstrates the God of Israel was one God head made of a plurality of entities within that Godhead. Deuteronomy 6:4, "Hear, O Israel: The LORD (Jehovah (pronounced yeh-ho-vaw') our God (elohiym) is one LORD (Jehovah).

It is important to understand that the Holy Spirit is truly God because of the fact that if we are born again He lives in us. What we allow ourselves to be part of we are inviting God to be part of. 1 Corinthians 6:19, "What, know ye not that your body is the temple of the Holy Ghost which is in you, which ye have of God, and ye."

As I stated previously, there are many scriptural references that prove the co-existence of the entities, or Persons, that make up the Holy Trinity. Right now, it is important for everyone to understand that there are three Persons, or individual entities, that are God being referred to as "God". An easy way to make everyone understand is to say; though there are many branches of a tree, the tree is still "a" tree; "one" tree having many branches. A family unit is made up of father, mother, and three children. Though there are five members of the family, it is "one" family; "one" unit.

The Holy Trinity, or Godhead is made up of three Persons, each one an individual; each termed "God". Together, they are one God even as the five that make up the family, one family, and the many branches that make up the tree, one tree.

There is a lot more to be said about the Holy Trinity and we will discuss it more in the coming pages.

Jesus spoke quickly when He saw they wanted to stone Him. He said, "I have shown you many good works from my Father. For which of those works would you stone me?"

The Jews replied, "We don't stone you for the good works you have done. We stone you for blasphemy; and," they added, "because you, being a man, make yourself God!"

Jesus answered, "If I do not the works of my Father, do not believe me. But if I do, though you believe not me, believe the works: that you may know, and believe, that the Father is in me, and I in him."

They sought, again, to take Jesus, but He escaped from them and went away beyond Jordan into the place where John first baptized and there abode. Here He spoke to those who would listen and many believed in Him.

*****

And while Jesus was in Jordan, Mary, which anointed the Lord with ointment, and wiped His feet with her hair, whose brother Lazarus was sick, sent servants to tell Him that he whom you love is sick.

When Jesus received the message, He turned to His disciples and said, "This sickness is not unto death, but for the glory of God, that the Son of God might be glorified."

Jesus loved Mary and her sister, Martha, and Lazarus. Nevertheless, Jesus did not go to Mary right away. Instead, He remained where He was for at least two days. After two days, He said to his disciples, "Come, we will go to Judaea again."

The disciples reminded Jesus, saying, "The Jews are looking to stone you! Why are you in such a hurry to go back there, again?"

Jesus replied, "… our friend Lazarus sleeps. I am going to awaken him out of his sleep."

A bit confused, Jesus' disciples said, "But if he is sleeping, Lord, it is good for him, is that not right?"

Jesus, than, spoke plainly and stated, "Lazarus is dead! I am glad for your sakes that I am not there so that you may believe that which you will see. Nevertheless," He added, "let us go to him."

And Then, Thomas, known as Didymus, looked to the other disciples and said, "Let us go that we may die with Him."

Die with whom? Was Thomas inferring that it would be a waste of time going to Judaea because Jesus had said that Lazarus was dead; and that because of the hostility against Jesus, they, too, could wind up dead, along with Lazarus? Or, was Thomas thinking that, surely, if Jesus goes to Judaea, He would be killed, and Thomas felt that if Jesus was stoned, he wanted to die with Jesus.

There are a great many things to consider when reading scripture and many options to cause one to wonder. Apparently, according to Jesus, Lazarus was already dead. Thomas, in this case had to be telling the other disciples that if Jesus was to be killed, he, as well as the other disciples (because they loved Jesus so much) would want to be killed with Him.

*****

By the time Jesus and his disciples arrived in Judaea, they found that Lazarus had been in the grave for four days. Lazarus' home was in Bethany, about fifteen furlongs from Jerusalem. A furlong is approximately an eight of a mile so Lazarus' home was less than 2 miles from the walls of Jerusalem.

Mary was in the house when Jesus arrived. But, Martha, her sister was outside mourning with their friends. When Martha saw Jesus approaching, she ran to meet Him, and fell at His feet, saying, "Lord, if you were here, my brother would not have died." Looking up at Jesus, with tears in her eyes, she continued, "but I know, that even now, whatever you ask of God, He will give it to you."

Looking down at Martha, Jesus said, "Your brother will live again."

"I know that he will live again, in the resurrection, at the last day," Martha exclaimed.

"*I* am the resurrection, and the life," Jesus replied. "He that believes in me, though he were dead, yet shall he live." Jesus paused, and then added, "And whosoever lives, and believes in me shall never die. Do you believe this, Martha?"

"I do, Lord!" Martha exclaimed. "I believe that you are the Christ, the Son of God, come into the world!" And when she had said this, she rose to her feet and hurried to call Mary, her sister, saying, "Mary! The Master is here and He wants to see you!"

Mary hurried to where Jesus was standing and fell at his feet, saying, "Lord, if you were here my brother would not have died!"

Jesus, then, upon seeing Mary and those who were with her crying was filled with compassion, groaned in the spirit, and was deeply troubled. Jesus wept.

When the Jews saw Jesus weeping, they murmured among themselves saying, "Look! Look how much He loved Lazarus!"

*****

But was Jesus weeping for Lazarus? Was He weeping because Lazarus was in the grave? Or, was He so filled with grief for Mary and Martha that He became emotional to the point of tears? The mere fact that "Jesus wept" tells us, most assuredly, that Jesus was as an ordinary man. Jesus made it clear to the world that He was both God and man. Only after the resurrection and in the generations to follow would the world know that Jesus was both God and man.

After Jesus had regained His composure, He moved away from Mary and Martha and approached the place where they had laid Lazarus. It was a cave and it was sealed closed by a huge stone that covered its entrance. Mary and Martha were directly behind Him.

The Son of God stood still for a little space; a few moments, and then turned to where Mary and Martha stood. "Take the stone away!" He commanded.

Mary and Martha looked into each other's eyes and Martha turned to Jesus and said, "Our brother has been dead for four days! By this time, he stinks!"

Jesus replied quickly, "Did I not tell you that if you believe you would see the glory of God?"

Martha signaled to those who were there to roll away the stone. After the stone had been rolled away, Jesus stood and prayed. And, at that time, it seemed as if nothing in the world was moving. No-one said a word but stood silently by; waiting to be witness to what was about to take place.

Then, Jesus turned his eyes towards the heavens and said, "Father... I thank you for hearing me." He paused a few seconds, and then added, "I know that you always hear me. But because of all these people who hear me, I said those words so that those who are here will believe that you've sent me." Jesus, then, looked at the opening in the cave and in a determined, commanding voice shouted, "Lazarus! Come forth!" And Lazarus came forth... even though he was bound with grave cloths, hand and foot, with a napkin over his face. Jesus shouted, "Loose him and let him go!"

Many of the Jews hurried to where Mary and Martha stood and all at once they believed in Jesus. At the same time many of the Jews hurried to tell the Pharisees what Jesus had done.

The Jews knew that the rulers of the temple did not approve of Jesus' ministry. And, while many of the Jews, after witnessing what He did; the miracles He performed, and the words He spoke, were beginning to believe in Jesus, others, in their hearts and minds just could not believe that Jesus was the Son of God, or, even that He was someone other than, perhaps, a prophet.

Prior to the coming of Jesus, there had been many others claiming to be the Son of God. They, by using trickery, and magic, convinced many Jews to follow them. But, after being threatened, they were quickly made to disappear, never to be heard of again.

The rulers of the temple; the High Priest, the Pharisees, Sadducees, and others didn't want Jesus around for a lot of reasons. To begin with, He was popular with the people and many of the things He taught them, like money changing in the temple, as well as the commercialization of religion that was very lucrative to the leaders in the temple, couldn't be permitted to continue. The rulers of the temple, also, did not want to draw too much attention to them; what with Jesus causing commotions, using innuendos that suggest to the Romans there was another King on earth other than Caesar. Many of the Jews in high offices were making too much money and didn't want anything to upset their apple carts, so to speak.

So, when many of the Jews witnessed Jesus raising Lazarus from the dead, many believed and accepted Jesus, and many hurried to Jerusalem to give the Pharisees the most recent news concerning Jesus and His miracles; as if Jesus had done something terrible.

And, when they heard the news, many of the chief priests, and the Pharisees, Scribes, and others got together in council. In discussing the situation they talked about how popular Jesus was becoming, the fact that He was doing more and more miracles and that if they let Him alone, all men would believe in Him, and the Romans would come and put a halt to their activities.

Caiaphas, the high priest at that time, interrupted their chaotic murmurings and individual conversations and exclaimed, "All of you know nothing!" He knew what he wanted to say and he had to be convincing, not only to those who wanted to be rid of Jesus for their own reasons, but for those who didn't want to offend a member of their own race having no evidence that Jesus was nothing more than a teacher, or a prophet, who loved the people and wanted to do good.

So, Caiaphas, sagaciously said, "Consider that it is expedient for us that one man should die for the people and that our whole nation does not perish." Caiaphas, and many of those subjected to his influence, wanted Jesus to die because of the reasons indicated. But, Jesus, essentially, was to die as the price for saving the nation as a whole. After all, it was Jesus who was causing all the commotion and even hurting their profits in the temple. Why shouldn't He be taken out of the picture? With Jesus gone, things would go back to how they were for everyone before He began to teach and perform his miracles. From that day on, their only concern was to put Jesus to death.

*****

"Love One Another"

*****

Chapter XI

Mary Anoints Jesus' Feet – Judas Objects
Jesus' Hour Had Come
Jesus Washes the Feet of the Disciples

It was six days before the Passover and Jesus went to Bethany. Mary and Martha prepared Him a supper and Lazarus, along with the disciples, sat with Jesus at the table. Mary, then, took a pound of very expensive ointment and anointed Jesus' feet and dried them with her hair. The disciples, and Lazarus, watched as Mary did this and the whole house was filled with the scent of the ointment.

Judas Iscariot, the disciple who would later betray Jesus, was infuriated and stood and said, "Why wasn't this ointment sold for three hundred pence and given to the poor?" (In US money, 20 pence would be worth about thirty cents (30). So, 300 pence would be about $4.50 in US Dollars).

John, the author of this gospel, interjects how he feels about Judas, probably while he was writing and not what his thoughts might have been when the event occurred. He states that Judas was not really annoyed because He felt the ointment used by Mary on Jesus' feet was wasted and that the poor would have benefited from the money they could have gotten for it, if sold. John herein is implying to his readers that Judas was, in fact, a thief and would have wanted the money for his self, and not for the poor. Judas was the disciple who was responsible for all the funds used by the disciples and Jesus in their travels.

Jesus calmed the situation by saying "Let her alone! The poor will always be with you, but I will not."

Many of the Jews knew that Jesus was in Bethany in the home of Lazarus and came, not only to see and hear Jesus;

they came, also, to see Lazarus whom Jesus raised from the dead. And, many of the chief priests, also, came and, while there, even consulted with each other about how they could put Jesus to death.

The following day when the Feast of the Passover began many Jews, knowing Jesus was coming to the feast, took branches of palm trees, and went out to meet him, shouting Hosanna; blessed is the King of Israel that comes in the name of the Lord!

And, Jesus came riding on a young ass, which is, in essence, a wild donkey. As Jesus came, the Jews threw the palm branches under the hooves of the ass and shouted Hosannas as He passed.

The Pharisees, when they saw how the people followed after Jesus became enraged and full of hate and bitterness for Him as they murmured to each other saying, "Do you see how the multitude is going after Him?"

Among the crowds of people shouting out praises and Hosannas to Jesus were those from other nations. Not only Jews chased after Jesus, but Greeks, also, who had come to worship at the feast. Some came specifically to find Jesus. They sought out Philip, Jesus' disciple, told him that they wanted to see Jesus.

Philip told Andrew and together they informed Jesus that the Greeks wanted to see Him and talk to Him. Jesus knew that all things pertaining to His mission was at a point where those who hated Him and wanted to see Him fail were coming to a head. This was when He looked at His disciples and told them, "The hour has come that the Son of Man should be glorified."

Jesus' tone suddenly became solemn and He spoke softly but as one with purpose and authority. He said, "Now is my soul troubled. But what shall I say? Shall I ask the Father to save me from this hour?" He looked directly into Andrew's eyes and continued, saying, "It is for this cause; this purpose that this hour is come. Father," He added, "glorify thy name."

At that precise moment, there came a voice from heaven, saying, "I have both glorified it and will glorify it again." Those who were standing by described it as a thundering voice or sound while others said an angel spoke to Him.

As the Son of God watched the multitude; some fearful of what would happen next, and others in awe, Jesus spoke quickly, saying, "The voice you have heard came not because of me but for your sakes! Now is the judgment of this world: now shall the prince of this world be cast out!" (Here, He was talking about himself and how He would be persecuted and put to death). Then, He said, "If I be lifted up from the earth I will draw all men to me." At this time, it was obvious that Jesus knew he would soon be put to death.

Those that were there and considered Jesus knew that the way He was talking signified His death and asked Him, saying, "The law teaches that Christ abides forever. Why are you saying that the Son of Man will be lifted up? Who is the Son of Man?"

To this, Jesus replied, "Yet a little while is the light with you. Walk while you have the light or darkness will come upon you: he that walks in darkness does not know where he is going. While you have the light, believe in it and you will be called the children of light." Then He departed and hid himself from the crowds.

*****

Jesus made it as clear as possible in all the things He said. He spoke of the light and was, in fact, telling the Jews that what He is teaching them was what the Father in heaven wanted them to learn. He spoke to them of the light. He told them to walk while there is light and told them that those who walk in darkness cannot know where they are going. "Do what I tell you," was what He was telling them and in doing so they cannot help but find their ways to eternal life. "On the other hand," He told them, "if you do not do as I say, you are not in the light; that is to say; you are walking in the dark and cannot possibly find your way into heaven." The light, as Jesus taught them is Him, and his teachings, and the darkness, in essence, is to ignore Him and not believe in Him. After all, has not Jesus repeatedly told the Jews that all He is, and all He does, comes from the Father?

Yet, even though Jesus had demonstrated the fact that He was divine; He made the lame to walk, the blind to see, and the deaf to hear. He healed those with palsy, cleansed the leper, and even raised the dead. Still, they did not believe in Him.

That the saying of Esaias the prophet might be fulfilled, which he spake, "Lord, who hath believed our report and to whom hath the arm of the Lord been revealed?"

Therefore they could not believe, because that Esaias said again, "He hath blinded their eyes, and hardened their heart; that they should not see with their eyes, nor understand with their heart, and be converted, and I should heal them." These things said Esaias, when he saw his glory, and spake of Him.

Nevertheless, there were some among the chief rulers who did believe in Jesus but were afraid to confess it for fear they would be put out of the synagogue. In fact, there were many among the chief rulers who believed in Jesus and though we do not know their names, we do know that Nicodemus and Joseph of Arimathea, in particular, believed that Jesus was the Son of God. These two members of the Sanhedrin were, of course, Pharisees. Yet, even though they were members of the Pharisaic Party, as were others who believed, they were too few and would not openly confess their belief in Jesus because, as stated above, they feared they would be put out of the synagogue.

Remember, also, that the Sadducees were the wealthy members of the Sanhedrin (the court system) who would never accept Jesus Christ as the Son of God based on reports they received concerning His teachings. The Sadducees, in essence, controlled the High Priest position and were influential in monetary matters of the temple even though the Pharisees were the rulers in the temple most respected by the people. But, even though the members of the Pharisees were "of the people" and those of moderate income, most of them were strict followers of the Mosaic Laws.

For even a member of the Pharisaic Party to say he liked Jesus and could reason that Jesus could be the Messiah; that could be blasphemy. The Pharisees had to concern themselves with what their position among the people would be as well as how ambitious they were. So, these are some of the reasons those of the Pharisaic Party did not openly say they believed in Jesus as the Son of God. Remember, Nicodemus visited Jesus by night, secretly.

*****

Jesus cried and said, "He that believeth in me, believeth not on me but on Him that sent me. He that sees me sees Him that sent me. I am come a light into the world that whosoever believes in me should not abide in darkness." He continued, obviously, speaking to His disciples. "... He that rejects me and does not receive my words, has one who will judge him: the word that I have spoken, the same shall be the judge on the last day." Jesus is telling the world that if His words are not received, these very things He taught would be the standards upon which the world will be judged.

Jesus continues, "For I have not spoken of myself, but the Father who sent me; He told me what I should say... what I should speak. And I know his words bring everlasting life. So, the words that I speak come from the Father. He commands me to speak, so I speak."

Please Note:

In many cases I have taken license to change words so as to make clearer what I believe what is written actually means. I have not changed the meaning of any thought, or lesson to be taught and the reader should, if possible, follow the Gospel of St. John to reassure himself of this. My objective in preparing this essay/novel is to present to the world the mission Jesus Christ came to accomplish. And, to do it in such a way so that everyone is able to understand. As I prepared this book, I have, also, found that there were many instances I would leave the text exactly as is written in the gospels and elsewhere. I have done my best to present this work without offering inferences, or innuendos.

*****

Now before the feast of the Passover, when Jesus knew that His hour was come that He should depart out of this world unto the Father, having loved His own which were in the world, He loved them unto the end. And, supper being ended, the devil having now put into the heart of Judas Iscariot, Simon's son, to betray Him.

Jesus, knowing that the Father had given all things into His hands, and that He was come from God, and went to God; He rose from supper, and laid aside his garments; and took a towel, and girded. After that He poured water into a basin, and began to wash the disciples' feet, and to wipe them with the towel wherewith He was girded. When it was time for Him to wash Peter's feet, Peter asked Jesus, "Will you also wash my feet?"

Jesus replied, "You do not understand, now, what I am doing, but you will in the future."

Peter would allow no such thing! He knew Jesus was the Son of God, and there was no way he was going to allow the Son of God to get down on his knees to wash his feet. And Peter exclaimed, "You will never wash my feet!"

Jesus replied, calmly, "If I do not wash your feet you will have no part of me."

Peter, than, understood what Jesus was doing. Instantly, he understood why his master was making such a gesture. If the Son of God, in all humility, gets on His knees to wash my feet, how much more should I humble myself in my service to all man-kind? He was telling me that the master is not greater than the servant. How much clearer could the Lord have made himself?

And Peter answered, "Wash not only my feet, but also my hands and my head." Peter, than knew that by Christ' example; he was called to be a humble servant to all men in the service of the Lord.

Jesus went on to say, "You are not all clean." He said this because He knew who was going to betray Him. After Jesus had finished washing the feet of His disciples, He dressed himself and sat down at the table and asked, "Do you know what I have done to you? You call me master and lord and you speak the truth, for I am. If I, your Lord and Master have washed your feet, you should also wash one another's feet. For I have given you an example; that you should do as I have done to you. So, I say unto you; the servant is not greater than his lord, and neither is He that is sent greater than He that sent him. If you know these things, you will be happy if you do them."

Jesus continued, "I speak not of you all: I know whom I have chosen: He that has eaten bread with me has lifted up his heel against me (Here, Jesus is talking about Judas who will betray him). I am telling you this before it happens so that when it does happen you will believe that I am the Christ. So, I say unto you, he who receives whomsoever I send unto you, receives me; he that receives me, receives Him that sent me."

Jesus, now, was troubled in the spirit and told His disciples, "Verily, verily, I say unto you, that one of you shall betray me."

When Jesus made the statement that one of His disciples would betray Him, it must have come as a shock to them. Not one of them could ever believe that any one of them would even think of doing such a thing. Every one of the disciples gave every indication of his love and loyalty to Jesus and some had openly stated that they would lay down their life for Him. The disciples looked at one another, doubting of whom He spoke.

Simon Peter, quickly, beckoned to the apostle who was leaning on Jesus' breast, referred to as the apostle whom Jesus loved (There is much to discuss concerning "the apostle whom Jesus loved", but I am not going to speculate and concern myself with this as I believe John, the author of this gospel, is he who is referred to) to ask Jesus the name of the apostle whom Jesus knew will betray Him. And, the apostle whom Jesus loved (Again, John) asked Jesus, "Lord, who is It?"

Looking at John, Jesus answered, "He it is, to whom I shall give a sop, when I have dipped it." And when He had dipped the sop, He gave it to Judas Iscariot, the son of

Simon.

*****

(You should know that the word, "artos" used in all of the gospel accounts for the bread eaten during the last supper is the Greek word for "bread". We, also, need to understand the "sop" itself.   This is the Greek word *psomion*, and means "a morsel," "a crumb," "a bit," "a fragment," or as Strong's interprets, "a mouthful." Thus, it means a piece of food, and in the Last Supper, one used particularly   for   dipping). http://www.cgg.org/index.cfm/fuseaction/Library.sr/CT/BQ A/k/221/Sop-Leavened-Unleavened-John-13-26-27.htm#ixzz1QCyHc19Q

And when He had dipped the sop, He gave it to Judas Iscariot, the son of Simon. And after the sop Satan entered into him. Then said Jesus unto him, "What you do, do quickly!"

So, what has happened here is; any good that was in Judas Iscariot quickly left him because Satan immediately took over his being.

Not one of Jesus' disciples seated at the table knew, or had any idea, why He had spoken to Judas as he had. Some of the disciples thought that, because Judas was in charge of their monies, he had been instructed to buy the things they needed for the feast; or, that he should give something to the poor. Judas, then, left immediately. The gospel indicates that it was night time.

Then, Jesus spoke, saying "Now is the Son of Man glorified. And, God is glorified in Him." (Here, Jesus is telling his disciples, and the world, that the time has come for Him to be glorified, and that God, the Father, will be glorified because of Him).

Jesus continues, "Little children, "I will be with you yet

a little while longer. You will look for me, but as I told the Jews; where I go, you cannot follow me, now. But, I tell all of you; a new commandment I give to you; you are to love one another. Even as I have loved you; love, also, one another. If you have love, one for another, then all men will know that you are my disciples."

Simon Peter leaned forward and asked, "Lord, where are you going?"

Calmly, and lovingly, Jesus replied, "Where I am going, you cannot come, now. But," he added, "You will follow me afterwards."

Peter said unto him," Lord, why cannot I follow you now? I will lay down my life for you."

Jesus quickly replied, "Will you lay down your life for me? I tell you this; you will deny me three times before the rooster even crows."   (In the Gospel of St. John, the account of the last supper makes no mention of Jesus taking the bread and wine and speaking of them as His body and blood. In the Gospels of Matthew, Mark, and Luke, Jesus takes the bread, breaks it, and blesses it, saying... This became the Institution of the Holy Eucharist).

The Eucharist (/'juːkərɪst/), also called Holy Communion, the Sacrament of the Altar, the Blessed Sacrament, the Lord's Supper, and other names, is a sacrament or ordinance that Christians celebrate in accordance with the instruction that, according to the New Testament, Jesus gave at His Last Supper to do in His memory what He did when He gave His disciples bread, saying, "This is my body", and wine, saying, "This is my blood".

Read more of the Last Supper as recorded by Sts.

Matthew, Mark, and Luke in <u>1 Corinthians 11:23-26</u> Apostle Paul provides the theological underpinnings for the use of the <u>Eucharist</u>, stating: For I received from the Lord what I also passed on to you: The Lord Jesus, on the night He was betrayed, took bread, [24]and when He had given thanks, He broke it and said, "This is my body, which is for you; do this in remembrance of me."

In the same way, after supper He took the cup, saying, "This cup is the new covenant in my blood; do this, whenever you drink it, in remembrance of me."

For whenever you eat this bread and drink this cup, you proclaim the Lord's death until He comes.

*****

The Last Supper

★★★★★

Chapter XII

Thomas Asks Jesus to Show Them the Father
Jesus Leaves the Comforter "Who Will Teach You All Things"
Jesus Commands Us to Love One Another

Jesus spoke softly, a smile on His face, "Let not your heart be troubled. You believe in God; believe, also, in me. In my Father's house are many mansions. If it were not so, I would have told you. I go to prepare a place for you. I will come again and receive you unto myself; that where I am, you may be also. And where I go, you know."

Just then, Thomas interrupted abruptly, saying, "Lord, we don't know where you are going. How can we?"

And Jesus responded by saying, "I am the way, the truth, and the life. No man comes to the Father but by me." He paused briefly, and then continued, "You say you know me, so you should know my Father, also. Because of this, you know Him, and you have seen Him." Jesus is telling Thomas and the other disciples that in seeing Him, they are seeing God the Father. He is not saying that He and God, the Father, are one, and the same person; He is saying that He and God are the same in purpose. He is saying that if you know Him (Jesus), and heard Him, you have seen God, and heard God because He, Jesus, does the Fathers will and exemplifies the Fathers love. Thomas wanted to be assured of God's presence in his life and in the life of all who believe in Jesus as the Son of God.

"Show us the Father" Philip said. "Show us and that will be enough!"

Jesus, now seeming to be a little annoyed with Thomas, replied, "Why is it that after being with me for so long, you still do not know me? He that has seen me has *seen* the

Father! Why do you ask me to show you the Father?" He paused, and then continued, "Don't you believe that I am in the Father, and the Father is in me? The words that I speak to you are not of myself: and the Father that dwells within me; He does the works! I tell you this; the works that I do, he shall do also; and greater works than these shall he do. I am going unto my Father. And, whatever you ask in my name, I will do so that the Father will be glorified in the Son. Whatever you ask in my name, I will do it if you love me and keep my commandments. I will pray to the Father, and He will give you another Comforter who will abide with you forever." (Here, of course, Jesus is telling his disciples not to worry when He is gone because He will ask the Father to send the Holy Spirit in His place. The Comforter is the Holy Spirit/Holy Ghost).

Jesus continues, "He will send you the Spirit of truth (The Holy Ghost) whom the world *cannot receive because the world cannot see Him so they can't know Him. But you know Him because He dwells with you and shall be in you."

He pauses, and then adds, "I will not leave you comfortless. I will come to you."

"The world cannot receive the Holy Ghost." Jesus is telling his disciples, and posterity that because the world cannot see him that they can't know him. He cannot be received as he, Jesus, was received, and will be received by millions all over the world because He, Jesus, came into the world as man; flesh and blood; for the purpose for which He was sent. Jesus was seen by man and lived as a man, and suffered and died as a man to reconcile humankind to God. The Holy Spirit, Jesus says, cannot be received because he cannot be seen.

"Yet a little while," Jesus adds, "and the world will see me no more. But you will see me. Because I live, you will live, also." Here, Jesus, knowing of his impending death, tells the disciples that it won't be long and He will be put to death. He tells his disciples that no-one, beyond when He will die, His glorification, and His ascension, will ever see Him again. (This does not mean that those who receive the gift of everlasting life won't see him. There is more to be said concerning this matter in the chapters to come). But, He tells his disciples that *they* will see Him again simply because He will return to them when He is resurrected. And, He tells them; because I will live, so will you. In essence, because of the resurrection; because of Jesus' victory over death, all can live again. This is the glory of God. (At the end of this work, I will explain in simple and easy to understand words exactly why Jesus came into the world, exactly what His mission was, and how we, God's children, fit into His plans.

"At that day," Jesus goes on to say, "you will know that I am in my Father, that you are in me, and that I am in you." (See preceding paragraph).

Then Judas (not Iscariot) asked Jesus, "How is it that you will manifest yourself unto us and not unto the world?"

This, of course, was a very good question and needed answering. The answer, as you will know, reassures the disciples of the Lord's never ending presence.

The Lord explained, "If a man loves me, he will keep my words, and my Father will love him, and we will come unto him, and live within him. He that does not love me will not keep my sayings. ... (Jesus, again, states that the words he speaks are not his but the Father's)."

Jesus goes on to say, "All the things I have said; all my sayings have been said while you were in my presence. But the Comforter, who is the Holy Ghost, whom the Father will send to you when I'm gone, in my name, will teach you all things. And, he, the Holy Ghost, will make you to remember all the things I have taught you.

"I leave with you my peace. I leave you with my peace; not the peace the world gives... my peace." With arms extended; a warm smile on his face, He adds, "Let not your heart be troubled; and don't be afraid. I have told you that I am going away and will come again. Rejoice if you love me because I am going unto the Father. Know, also, that my Father is greater than I. I have told you all of these things so that when they come to pass you will believe." He paused and sighed, and then said, "From here-on we will not talk much. Hereafter, the world will know that I love the Father. He has commanded me to do that which I will do. Come, let us go."

*****

Above, Jesus has given his farewell to his disciples, and ended with telling them that because He loves the Father, he will do as He was commanded to do. Obviously, it was planned that Jesus would exit the world by God's command. He was prepared to obey what God had commanded, and that was to give His life for the remission of all sin. He assured His followers, His disciples, that they would not be alone once He had been sacrificed. He told them He would return to them and that, thereafter, He would leave them with the Holy Ghost who would assist them by bringing to them all remembrance of the things He had taught them. He told them not to be afraid because He would always be with them. They would be assisted by the Comforter who is the Holy Ghost so, He told them, in essence, not to worry and "let not your hearts be troubled'.

Jesus wanted them to be at peace, one with the other, and with themselves. He told them that the peace He would leave them would not be the kind of peace the world offered. He left them with *His* peace. He left them with the peace of the Son of God; the King of Kings. He left them with the kind of peace that could only come from one who teaches that a person, if struck on one cheek, should offer the other, also. He left with His disciples the kind of peace that prepares any and all who have it to give their all, even their life, to preserve such a peace. These are the things Jesus Christ was sharing with His disciples when He knew He was going to die.

Jesus was telling His disciples a great deal more. He told them that there was a place for them, with Him, in His Father's house and that He was on His way there to prepare a place for them so that they could be with Him. He spoke of all the things the disciples needed to hear because, indeed, they were afraid. When Philip suggested that Jesus show them the Father, he was no doubt looking for assurance from Jesus that He was divine; He was a part of the father; He was the Son of God. Jesus scolded Philip, gently, telling him that he should know that the Father was in Him (Jesus), and that He (Jesus) was in the Father. In other words; how could Philip not know this, having been with Jesus such a long time?

He told them to love one another as he loved them. He gave a simple but emphatic demonstration by washing the disciples' feet so that they would always remember that the master is not greater than the servant. He was teaching the disciples humility, and love, loyalty, and devotion; one towards the other. He let the whole world know that the Father in heaven does not distinguish between those who are the rich and those who are the poor; those who are educated and those who are foolish; royalty or peasant, and anyone else. He emphasized that all are equal in the eyes of the Father. These are the things Jesus wanted to leave his disciples with; all the things they would, with the help of the Holy Ghost, teach the world, which was the reason Christ chose them.

*****

Even though it would have been obvious to any individual who could have been present at the last Passover the disciples spent with Jesus that Jesus was going to die soon, it seems as though the disciples still did not understand that the Lord wasn't just going away someplace to hide, or vacation, or just disappear.

In much of the 15th chapter of the Gospel of St. John, Jesus seems to be telling them much of what He told them in Chapter 14. But, He does tell them, also, "I am the true vine and my Father is the husbandman." This, of course, means that the Father (God) is the one who takes care of the vine, or garden. The husbandman is generally known as the person who takes care of the garden and oversees the production of fruits, and vegetable in the garden.

"Every branch in me that does not bear fruit is taken away: and every branch that bears fruit, he purges it, that it may bring forth more fruit."

Jesus, now, goes on to explain what he meant by vine and bearing fruit. He explains, "I am the vine, you are the branches: He that abides in me and I in him, the same brings forth much fruit: for without me you can do nothing. If a man does not abide in me, he is cast forth as a branch, and is withered; and men gather them, and cast them into the fire, and they are burned. If you abide in me, and my words abide in you, you shall ask what you will, and it shall be done unto you. My Father will be glorified if you bear lots of fruit. And, if you bear much fruit, you are my disciples."

*****

Before I proceed, I should remind my readers that what Jesus is saying to his disciples, he is, in fact, saying to the world and those who would believe in him thousands of years later. He told his disciples that the Holy Ghost will bring all things He said, and taught them, to their remembrance. He told them this for a reason.

The disciples, we know, were chosen by Jesus, and were taught by him so that they would continue Jesus' work when he was no longer with them. In other words; you need not worry. He let them know that, in truth, he and the Father would not let them forget what Jesus wanted the world to know about him, and what was required of mankind, in order for them to please God. So, Jesus was teaching them all things that are explained in this book.

The majority of Jesus' disciples had little education to speak of. Simon who was later surnamed Peter, and his brother Andrew, were tough, coarse rough fisherman before they met Jesus. James and his brother John were sons of Zebedee - a fisherman in the days when life expectancy was only around 45. This meant that if Zebedee was still an active fisherman, and, therefore, still young, James and John would be no more than teenagers when they met Jesus. They probably would not have had a career at that time, although it is probable that they would have followed in their father's footsteps and become fishermen themselves. Matthew (Levi) was a hated tax collector. Tax collectors were hated, as they were in cahoots with the Roman occupying army and collected money for them. They often swindled their own countrymen to make a lot more money than they were paid by the Romans. On hearing Jesus call to him "follow me" we are told that Matthew left his booth there and then and followed him, never to return to his evil ways.

Simon the Zealot, from Canaan, as his name implies was a political activist who wanted to see the Romans out of Judaea. Other than that little is recorded in the gospels about him. Judas Iscariot was the 'keeper of the purse' (i.e., the treasurer) of the 12 disciples. Some have inferred from this that he had a previous life to do with accountancy, but there is no evidence in the gospels of this. Thomas was called 'Didymus' meaning 'a twin'. Therefore he had a twin brother somewhere but he is not recorded in the gospels. As for the other disciples, Philip, James the son of Alpheus, Bartholomew and Thaddeus we are not told about them before they met Jesus. Nor are we told anything about Matthias, the apostle chosen to replace Judas Iscariot after his suicide out of remorse for betraying Jesus.

The only other 'apostle', Paul, was not one of the 12 but is still regarded as an apostle as he met the risen Christ on the Damascus Road, and founded many churches across the Roman Empire. Paul was born in Tarsus, on the south coast of Turkey and was both a Jew and a Roman citizen. He was a tent-maker by trade. Paul was also trained in Jewish law by the great teacher Gamaliel and became a high-ranking Jewish official and Pharisee in Jerusalem. Before his conversion to follow Christ, he was a persecutor of Christians, and we are told that he (using the Jewish version of his name (Saul) was present when Stephen, the first Christian martyr, was stoned to death for his faith, and looked on with approval.

Apart from Paul, who was highly educated, the others would have had a basic education in the Mosaic Law and in their Hebrew faith. This does not mean to say that they were unintelligent - those who went on to write Biblical books (like the letters of Peter and John, and the gospels of Matthew and John) showed a high degree of intelligence -

but they would not have had the sort of education that we would take for granted today.

Nevertheless, Jesus saw qualities in all of these people that many others missed - qualities that, with the help of the Holy Spirit, turned them from a motley crew into the greatest evangelistic team that the world has ever known.

*(The information above was taken from: http://wiki.answers.com/Q/What_were_the_disciples_like_before_they_met_Jesus#ixzz1QVSOxMYW. To learn more about the disciples, visit this web site).

*****

I am not inferring that the original disciples were ignorant or difficult to teach, or anything of the sort. The Lord Jesus did not tell them the Holy Ghost would be sent only to help them to remember all the things he taught them. Simply put; the Holy Ghost would be sent to the disciples to comfort them, _and_ to aid them through life's trials and difficulties. And, because every one of us, brilliant or foolish, is only a man, and not God, we forget things and, often times, find it difficult to remember every detail concerning things of importance. The Holy Ghost, among other things, would, as Jesus said, "But the Comforter, which is the Holy Ghost, whom the Father will send in my name, he shall *teach* you all things, _and_ bring all things to your remembrance, whatsoever I have said unto you."

*****

Jesus spoke again, saying, "As the Father has loved me, so have I loved you. Continue in my love."

The disciples listen attentively as Jesus explains, "Greater love has no man than that a man lays down his life for his friends."

Not one of his disciples said anything when Jesus said

this. In this statement, the Lord is talking about a love one has for another that is so great that the one would die for the other. It is, of course, a statement so profound; still not one of his followers asked the simple question, "what does He mean?" or, "what is He telling us?"

While it is true the disciples loved Jesus and openly declared their willingness to give their life for Him, it seemed as if they still had no idea of what their master was telling them. During this gathering it should have been obvious to them that Jesus was talking about his impending death. The disciples seemed to be oblivious to what Jesus was teaching them. This gathering, it seems; at least to me; it was a long farewell address during which Jesus repeatedly said the same things again and again.

In considering all things, i.e.; the disciples' ability to understand and comprehend and, when they were able to come to any kind of an understanding; were they understanding the way Jesus wanted them to understand?

In essence, Jesus called these men who were uneducated, simple, and hard-working because of this. Jesus wanted those who were common, plain men who loved God.

When Jesus chose the twelve, he wasn't looking for those who were handsome, or rich, or influential. He was looking for real, God fearing men, who would be willing to learn from Him and, eventually offer their lives, as well.

Jesus knew everything He wanted to know about those He chose to be his disciples. He knew their weaknesses, and their strengths. He knew that Peter would deny Him, and He knew that Judas would betray Him. There was nothing about them He didn't know. The most important thing He knew about the men He chose was their potential. He knew that, eventually, after He was gone and the Holy Ghost descended upon them; they would be most effective in carrying on His work and establishing His church. These men, holy, loyal, and devoted to Christ would come to understand in due time. Jesus knew this.

*****

Jesus went on to command them to love each other. And, about them, He says, "You have not chosen me; I have chosen you, and ordained you, that you should go and bring forth fruit, and that your fruit should remain. And, whatsoever you shall ask of my Father in my name, He shall give you."

*****

Jesus made it very clear to the world in telling the disciples that He 'ordained' them, after He chose them. The word 'ordained' as it is used in God's Word, means that the ones ordained were 'appointed' by God to carry on in His name. In the biblical sense; anyone who feels called or chosen to serve the Lord is 'ordained' by Him to do his work.

To be ordained by man is not the same as to be ordained by God. Moses, in being chosen by God to lead the Hebrews out of Egypt, was, indeed, 'ordained' by God and given a mission. He was appointed to do what God chose him to do. The same applies to Jeremiah, Isaiah, Daniel, David, Saul (Paul). And, Jesus told these men, chosen and 'ordained', to go and bring forth fruit... fruit that would remain. The word 'fruit' herein means souls who would be steadfast in their love and devotion to the church/Christ. Their mission would be to win souls for Christ who would, in turn, do the same. This is what Jesus meant when He told his disciples to bring forth fruit (that is to say, "be fruitful").

In today's world, in order to be ordained by man, by a specific church, one would have to be acquainted with, and agree with, that particular church's 'sacraments', 'rules and regulations', what they say they believe, and everything else they say one must adhere to that would be specified in its charter. Many churches have rules concerning celibacy, marriage (they tell you who you can and cannot marry), how much of your earnings you must tithe the church, etc., to name but a few items. Even though you tell them, emphatically, that you were called by God; if you do not "qualify" or accept what they state is "truth", they; the church council (men), will not 'ordain' you.

"He shall feed his flock like a shepherd: he shall gather the lambs with his arm, and carry them in his bosom, and shall gently lead those that are with young". Isaiah 40:11
*****

Also, when an individual is ordained by God, rest assured that that person had been chosen to do something specific for Him. In choosing an individual to carry out a mission, God makes no mistake concerning his choice. So, when such a person is chosen by God, he is "ordained" and, ultimately, completes the mission.

Now, when men choose an individual for ordination, many times it could be a mistake. That is to say; men, because they are not "God", do err. Often, we have heard, or know of one who was ordained a priest who left the priesthood to be married; or for some other reason. Not only priests have put aside their vows, but others, also, for one reason or another.

So, when a person says he is "called" to be a priest or minister, it is not the same thing as being "chosen". When God chooses an individual, because God does not make mistakes, that person continues in His service. The other who is "called" might or might not continue to serve.

Chapter XIII

God's World Is One of Love and Humility
The Holy Ghost Will Guide You to the Truth
Jesus asks, "Do you now believe?"

Jesus tells the disciples that they are His friends as long as they do as He commands. "You are my friends," He says, "if you do whatsoever I command you." This, of course, sounds like an ultimatum. In other words; He is telling the disciples that if they do not do as He commands they are not his friends? Of course not! I believe that Jesus is telling them that if they do what He commands, He will always be with them and their lives will be blessed. Whereas if they disregard His commandments; that is to say; if they stray from His teachings for whatever reason, they will not receive the blessings and the Holy Ghost will leave them.

He states directly that the world will hate them but that they should know that the world hated Him before it will begin hating them. "If you were of this world, the world would love you. But," He adds, "because I have chosen you and you are not of this world; the world hates you."

Jesus is telling His disciples that the world of God is a world of love and humility. God's world is a world of respect for our neighbors, peace, equality for all, truth and obedience to Him and the things He teaches.

What Jesus is talking about when He says the disciples are not of this world is the fact that the things of the "world" are sinful (those things that are contrary to his teachings and the Ten Commandments), and the disciples, who have no part in the sinful things are not part of the world. To be part of the world, the disciples would be living a life that is just the opposite of how Christ expects them to live. Those who are part of the world would be indifferent, greedy, lustful (lascivious), full of bigotry, hateful, revengeful, deceitful, untruthful, dishonest, scornful, obese, and adulterous.

The disciples, Christ is saying, cannot be a part of the world. It is to be their mission to preach and teach the world that to be a part of the world is sinful. Not to be a part of the world is to be righteous (full of love for ones fellow man). And, because they, the disciples, are not part of the world, those who hear them will hate them. It will not be easy for the disciples, Jesus is saying. He was telling them what to expect throughout their ministry.

Jesus continues by telling His followers that the servant is not greater than his lord. So, He says, "If they persecuted me, they will, also, persecute you. But," He adds, "If they heard me and keep my sayings, they will also hear you and abide by my teachings."

Jesus, then, continues to tell the disciples that the things they (the world... the unrighteous) will do to persecute them will really be meant against Him. And, Jesus implies; they (the world) would be doing their works of persecution because they don't really know God (his Father). The world, Jesus is saying, is full of hate for Him.

"If I had not come and spoken unto them, they had not had sin: but now they have no cloak for their sin," Jesus said. He sighed, than added, "He that hates me hates the Father, also.

"If I had not done among them the works which none other man did, they had not had sin: but now have they both seen and hated both me and my Father."

*****

In the two verses of scripture above Jesus explains to the disciples that because He came into the world and taught the Jews, and told them what God requires of them, there is no excuse for their sins; their disobedience to His Father. He told His followers that, now, the Jews, and all who heard Him cannot argue ignorance as something to hide behind. He explained to His followers that the works (the miracles) He performed among them; the things He had done that no other man had done should be evidence of His relationship with His Father. But, He told them, it was to no avail because he ended by saying, "but now they have both seen and hated both me and my Father."

*****

Gospel of St. John, as one can easily determine, is not written as is the Gospels of Matthew, Luke, and Mark. In the aforementioned gospels, one can read the parables that Jesus spoke, and learn of the many miracles he performed, as well of several times when he brought the dead to life.

This gospel, the Gospel of St. John, concentrates mostly on what Jesus wanted us to know about him and God, the Father.

Unlike the synoptic gospels, those mentioned above, John's account of Jesus seems to be as though He, Jesus, is in a classroom, like a teacher, and the disciples are His students in a school, which is the "world".

There is a great deal of controversy concerning who the author of the Gospel of St. John really was. The gospel is closely related in style and content to the three surviving Epistles of John such that commentators treat the four books together, yet according to most modern scholars John was not the author of any of these books.

Raymond E. Brown did pioneering work to trace the development of the tradition from which the gospel arose. The discourses seem to be concerned with the actual issues of the church-and-synagogue debate at the time when the Gospel was written *c.* AD 90. It is notable that, in the gospel, the community still appears to define itself primarily *against* Judaism, rather than as part of a wider Christian church. Though Christianity started as a movement within Judaism, gradually Christians and Jews became bitterly opposed.

John presents a "higher" Christology than the synoptic, meaning that he describes Jesus as the incarnation of the divine Logos (Word) through whom all things were made, as the object of veneration, and more explicitly as God incarnate.

Only in John does Jesus talk at length about himself and his divine role, often shared with the disciples only. Against the synoptic gospels, John focuses largely on different miracles (including resurrecting Lazarus), given as signs meant to engender faith.

Synoptic elements such as parables and exorcisms are not found in John. It presents a realized eschatology in which salvation is already present for the believer. According to the majority viewpoint, the synoptic gospels are more historically reliable than John.

The Gospel of John developed over a period of time in various stages, summarized by Raymond E Brown as follows:

1. An initial version based on personal experiences of Jesus;

2. A structured literary creation by the evangelist which draws upon additional sources;

3. The final harmony that presently exists in the New Testament canon, around 85-90 AD.

The Gospel of John is closely related in style and content to the three surviving Epistles of John such that commentators treat the four books together, yet according to most modern scholars John was not the author of any of these books.

You can read more about the Apostle John and make your own decision concerning authorship by visiting www.wikipedia.org/the gospel of John. I am not concerned about who the author was or is. Rather, I am only concerned about the content, as all of us should be. As I stated previously, only in John does Jesus talk at length about himself and his divine role, often shared with the disciples only. I wanted to explain why I did not include those things such as parables and the many events concerning Jesus' miracles while at the same time discuss a little about how the book might have come about and approximately when it was written.

*****

There were times when Jesus wanted to be alone so He could pray and meditate. Often He would think about His earthly father, Joseph, whom He loved very much. He would, also, think about Thomas, His childhood companion. He really missed seeing his friend though, a few times, while in Bethany, He went out of His way to visit Thomas and his family.

The last time Jesus was able to visit Thomas and his wife, Arella; He was accompanied by His disciples. Thomas was glad to meet them and welcomed Jesus and His followers with opened arms. He and His wife were happy for the opportunity to prepare food for them, after which Thomas had many questions about Jesus' ministry he wanted to know and try to understand.

Of course, Thomas had heard about how Jesus raised Lazarus from the dead, and how He cured others of their diseases and infirmities. He spent hours sitting and talking with Jesus about Jesus' ministry. Thomas thought he knew his friend but soon discovered that Jesus had become someone who was different from the Jesus he grew up with.

Yes, Jesus was always telling the truth and He never said anything to hurt any of the others' feelings. Jesus always knew more than anyone else about the scriptures, even the Rabbi's. But, now that Jesus is a man, and is traveling with those He calls his disciples, Thomas recognized a "holy" kind of an atmosphere when in His presence. He recognized all the attributes that anyone who knew anything at all about people *should* recognize. Jesus, Thomas determined, is loving, humble, and caring. Thomas was afraid of what could happen to Jesus because he had heard reports out of Jerusalem about the many enemies Jesus had and how they might look to have Him killed.

But, when Jesus had the good fortune to be able to visit Thomas, it was always a, mostly, happy occasion. Jokes would be told and Jesus enjoyed being around Thomas' children. Jesus, himself, even told jokes and laughed and took time to play with the kids.

Jesus was very happy when he visited his friend, Thomas. And, Thomas loved Jesus and Mary, His mother, so much that he offered to build a home for Jesus and Mary and give Him custodial charge of his vineyards. But, as much as Jesus loved Thomas bar Abbas, it was out of the question, of course. Jesus knew who He was and that He had a mission to accomplish for His Father, in heaven.

Many of Jesus' thoughts were pleasant and wonderful. Jesus, because He was, besides being God, a man, had dreams just like any other man. Like any other man, Jesus slept and, I am sure He had dreams like other men.

However, Jesus was both God and man and didn't think as men do. Though He had feelings, and experienced

137

pain, and all the other things others go through, He, being God thought as God thinks concerning worldly things.

Jesus had to be different when it came to mind and spirit. He had to be perfect as a man concerning these things, specifically. He had to be perfect in this respect or how could He be the price paid to His Father for the sins of the world?

Some might have suggested that He could have dreamt about women and other things of the world simply because He was a man. I don't believe He ever had such dreams and, to me, such a suggestion would be ludicrous. If anyone could believe that the Son of God could think things that are worldly, e.g.; they would be suggesting that He was not divine in nature and, therefore, could not truly accept Him as being the Son of God.

Remember, Jesus is God incarnate. He is God become man. On earth, while carrying on with His mission, He was, at the time, a divine being among all other men. A man on a mission that had to be accomplished for the sake of his Father and His children, lest they be lost which all would have been, had he not come to earth to pay the price.

*****

"Because you identify with me and my Father, they will put you out of the synagogues," Jesus said. "And, the time will come when whoever kills you; that person will be thinking he did God a good service.

They will do these things to you because they have no knowledge of the Father, or me. Again, I tell you these things now so that when they happen, you will remember that I told you.

"But now I must go back to Him that sent me and not one of you has asked me where I am going. Still, because I tell you these things, I can see how full of sorrow you are.

But, it is true when I tell you that it is expedient for you that I go away. If I do not go away, the Holy Ghost will not come to you. If I go away, I will send him unto you."

Jesus sighed, spoke softly, and added, "I have so many things I have yet to say to you but you cannot bear them now. When the Spirit of truth comes (the Holy Ghost) He will guide you into all that is truth. He will not speak of Himself and will show you all the things that are to come.

He will take to task the world of sin, of righteousness, and of judgment. He will glorify me through you because of the things I have shown you. Everything that the Father has is mine. I have told you that the Holy Ghost shall take from me and give it to you. Because of this I will be glorified."

*****

Jesus is explaining to His followers that He has so much more to teach them but not to worry because when the Holy Ghost comes upon them, He will guide them to truth. Jesus tells them that the Holy Ghost will not be with them to talk about Himself; He will talk about what is happening and show them all the things to come. By doing this, the Holy Ghost will guide and show them the way that they, best, can do the work they had been chosen by God to do.

*****

Again, Jesus says, "A little while, and ye shall not see me: and again, a little while, and ye shall see me, because I go to the Father." (He knows He will be crucified and He knows He will return and then later return to His Father in heaven).

Some of the disciples murmured among themselves, saying, "What is He talking about: a little while?" It seems obvious that the disciples were confused. They still couldn't understand where Jesus was going with what He was saying.

"Now, you are feeling sorrow. But, I will see you again and your hearts will rejoice with joy, and no man will be able to take it from you. And, when that day comes you will ask nothing of me. But, whatever you shall ask the Father in my name, he will give it to you. Ask and you shall receive that your joy may be full."

Jesus, now, goes on to tell them, "I came from my Father and came into the world: now I leave the world and will go back to my Father."

Bothered by what Jesus is saying, His disciples exclaimed, "Speak plainly!" We are now sure that you know all things. We now believe that you came from God."

Finally! It took the disciples several years to conclude that Jesus came from God. To them, now; Jesus wasn't just some prophet or teacher like many others who came before Him. They concluded, finally, that Jesus came from God. Thus, they concluded that Jesus is divine. He is the Son of God!

For such a long time, they heard Him teach using parables; they watched as He opened blind eyes, unstopped deaf ears, made the lame walk, cleansed the leper, fed thousands of people with a few fish and a couple of loaves of bread; They watched as He raised the dead! And, now, finally, the disciples told Him, "We now believe that you came from God!"

To this, Jesus replied, as if being so frustrated for so long; "Do you now believe?"

(It seems odd that Jesus, here, would make it appear that He had finally been convinced that His disciples accepted Him as the Son of God when on another occasion Peter had declared in no uncertain terms that Jesus was the Christ).

In this same gospel, we read, "Then Simon Peter answered him, Lord, to whom shall we go? Thou hast the words of eternal life. *And we believe and are sure that thou art that Christ, the Son of the living God"* St. John 6:68, 69. In this scripture, Peter is saying "we". Surely, the apostles/disciples talked amongst themselves concerning the subject and, by Peter's declaration, he was speaking for the group. Why Jesus appears to be free from frustration regarding how the disciples finally accepted Him is confusing.

One could say that what Peter declared is altogether different than what the disciples said, "We now believe that you came from God." It is true that what Peter said in John 6:69 means exactly as it appears. "We believe and are sure that thou art that Christ, the Son of the living God."

One could not misinterpret that statement. When the disciples finally concluded that they believe that Jesus came from God; it could mean that, as Moses, Isaiah, and Jeremiah came from God, so did Jesus? The only way I can interpret the disciples saying they believe Jesus came from God is:

They meant to imply that Jesus is the Christ. Or, they finally really and truly, now, believe that Jesus is the Christ. Jesus, being God, may have known that the time had come when *all* understanding finally dawned on the disciples and, though they may have *faintly* believed Jesus was the Son of God before; now, there is no doubt).

"Behold, the hour has now come," Jesus exclaimed, "that you shall be scattered; every one of you to your own place. Even though you will be away from me, I will not be alone because my Father is with me.

"I have told you all these things hoping that you might have peace." Jesus paused for a couple of seconds and then continued, "In the world, you will have tribulation. But be of good cheer because I have overcome the world."

*****

Jesus, the Master, King of Kings, the Good Shepherd, the Son of Man, or, Son of God; Jesus, the Savior and Redeemer of mankind had just finished his "group" lesson to the disciples.

But, it is believed that as many as thirteen individuals were present and, maybe even seventy (70), or more. No-one really knows the exact number of those present, but, let me explain this way: "Thirteen people attended the Last Supper. Jesus had 12 disciples."

This is not necessarily true, at least in part - Jesus had 12 *apostles* that is, His closest followers; inner circle. He actually had at least 70 disciples (Luke 10:1) and probably very many more than that. Remember that when the 11 remaining apostles chose a replacement for Judas after his suicide, they cast lots to decide among those followers who had been with them the whole time (Acts 1:20-26). (They had chosen Matthias).

In terms of the last supper, in Mark 14:13 Jesus sends two of His disciples off to find a venue, and then later arrives with the twelve [apostles]; there is no suggestion that the two who went ahead were from the twelve, and so they, at least, would probably have joined Him for the supper in addition to the apostles.

In the English translation of the text in Mark, Jesus uses two separate phrases: "disciples" and "the twelve", suggesting that at least some non-apostle disciples were there with Him. In addition, Jesus was known to have a number of women in His entourage (Luke 8:1-3, amongst other references) and it is incredibly unlikely that these women followers would not have served at the supper.

It is, of course, pretty unlikely that there would not have been 70 or so followers with Jesus for dinner, but the gospel accounts certainly allow for there to be more than 13 of them, and it is highly likely that at least some of His female disciples were there in addition to the 12 apostles.

(Most of the above information concerning how many people were present at the last supper was taken from Wikipedia Free Library wherein are scriptural facts that are inconclusive regarding this subject). But, as indicated above, the gospel accounts certainly allow for there to be more than 13 of them, and it is highly likely that at least some of his female disciples were there in addition to the 12 apostles.

Read more by visiting:
http://wiki.answers.com/Q/How_many_people_attended_Jesus'_Last_Supper#ixzz1QrssB3v5bvisitinhttp://wiki.answers.com/Q/How_many_people_attended_Jesus'_Last_Supper#ixzz1QrssB3v5 and the scriptures

Jesus told all of those who were present that they will have tribulation. That is to say; they would be persecuted; they would suffer. "But be of good cheer," He added, "because I have overcome the world."

In this verse of scripture, Jesus was somewhat like a cheer leader who wanted to motivate and inspire those who were present. On the one hand, Jesus laid it all out, truthfully, and in no uncertain terms. He told them they would be persecuted. He made it clear to them that they, being not of the world, would be ridiculed and persecuted for his sake, by the world. But, He added, that they should be brave because He, Jesus, had "overcome" the world. He was telling them that in spite of the persecution they would have to endure there would be peace, joy, and happiness, everlastingly, for them because *He* had "overcome the world".

In the synoptic Gospels, Matthew, Mark, and Luke, you can read the parables Jesus spoke that were used to teach and explain the benefits and rewards, as well as the "requirements" set forth by Him in order for all of us to be inheritors/worthy of these rewards, and benefits.

In essence, Jesus was teaching the world that to be "of this world" one is not worthy of the blessings and the gift of life everlasting an individual who is "not of this world" receives. (Read, also, Paul's letter to the Romans, as well as Peter's letters, Hebrews, and the other epistles wherein lie all the requirements a Christian must meet In order to find favor with God).

Jesus, by His suffering, death, and, by His resurrection has overcome the world. With the fulfillment of the prophets, and by the shedding of His blood for the sins of the world; by His victory over death; He has overcome.

*****

Praise the Lord!

*****

Chapter XIV

"God's plan of salvation"
Judas' Betrayal of Christ
Jesus in the Garden of Gethsemane

"O Father, glorify thou me with thine own self with the glory which I had with thee before the world was." Here, in prayer, Jesus is asking his Father to glorify Him as He was glorified even before the world was. By this, we have Jesus' own confirmation that He was with the Father before the world was created. And, He is asking his Father to restore the glory He had because He had just about completed the task He came to earth to accomplish.

He says, "I have manifested thy name unto the men which *you have given me* out of the world: they are yours, and *you gave them to me*; and they have kept thy word." This is to say: those who were chosen; the apostles, the disciples, and others *were already known to God and Christ before they were chosen to be apostles and disciples, and followers who would carry on after Jesus' sacrifice*. He said, "I have made known thy name to the men *you gave me* and they have kept your word.

Jesus, now, tells God that "I have given unto them the words which you gave me; and they have received them, and have known surely that I came out from thee, and they have believed that thou didst send me."

In other words, Jesus taught the apostles and the others *what God wanted Him to teach*. He is assuring God that those He taught, His apostles, and disciples, concluded that He was from God and believed He was sent from above (God). We here learn that all that has happened with Christ and those He taught, and what Christ taught, was *part of a divine plan* designed to save those who would otherwise perish, at death. It is to be known as *"God's plan*

145

of salvation" for all mankind. (In my final remarks, I will talk more of what Jesus' crucifixion (his death) on the cross really means to every person on the earth who has ever lived, is now alive, and who will live until the final day).

*****

Jesus, then, says, "And now I am no more in the world, but these are in the world." He knows his time has come and He has already acknowledged to his Father his impending death. He is telling his Father that, though He is no longer in the world, these (his disciples) are in the world. He asks God to bless and keep them that they may be one as He and his Father are one.

Then Jesus tells his Father, God, how he was with those whom the Father had given to Him and tells of how not one of them were lost but the son of perdition (referring to Judas Iscariot), "so that the scripture is fulfilled."

Who was the son of Perdition? Judas Iscariot, one of the chosen twelve apostles. He appeared to be loyal and devoted to Jesus, and for all anyone knew, he was. Judas was intelligent and conducted himself in a business-like manner. He was *so* trusted, and business-like; and, he was so intelligent; he was chosen to "hold the bag", if you will. He was the treasurer.

However, even though the apostles trusted Judas, Jesus, being fully aware of the character of those who followed Him, knew that Judas was stealing from them. I refer you to this same gospel wherein it is written, *"This (Judas) said, not that he cared for the poor; but because he was a thief, and had the bag, and bear what was put therein."*

Why then did Jesus, if knowing Judas' character, and, realizing he (Judas) was taking money that was not his, allow Judas to continue in his capacity as treasurer? I

146

really cannot offer any reasonable explanation as to why Jesus and the other followers kept Judas with them. Some would suggest that Jesus wanted to allow Judas the time to "fight the good fight". In other words; would Judas be able to overcome the temptation he faced every day as "holder of the bag"?

To fight against temptation and to overcome it is to build good character. Victory over temptation is victory over Satan; and winning over Satan would make one stronger in the faith and, consequently, more effective as a follower of Jesus. Others could think of even other reasons why Jesus would allow Judas to remain one of his apostles since He had others He could have chosen.

The Prophet Zechariah prophesied the betrayal of Jesus hundreds of years before the event. 'If it is good in your sight, give me my wages, but if not never mind!' So they weighed out thirty pieces of silver as my wages. Then the Lord said to me, it to the potter, that magnificent price at which I was valued by them.' So I took the thirty shekels of silver and threw them to the potter in the house of the Lord" (Zechariah 11:12, 13 NASB).

While scholars and learned theologians offer many reasons as to why Judas was permitted to remain, I don't agree with any of them other than the fact that he (Judas) was part of the plan of salvation which would, ultimately, lead to Christ' death on the cross, and the resurrection. Very simply put, God had a plan for the salvation of all men. It wasn't a plan that Jesus was to make up as He went along. We are told that God knew who would be chosen by Jesus to carry out his plan of salvation. Jesus makes this clear to the entire world when He said, "I have manifested thy name unto the men which *you have given me* out of the world: they are yours, and *you gave them to me*; and they have kept thy word." What could be clearer than this?

Jesus knew that Judas was a "thief" as the scriptures tell us. And, He also knew that Judas was the one who would betray Him.

The betrayal of Christ by the prophets is clear and since He had utilized the men which were given Him by his Father *who gave them to Him*, the only reason for Judas being one of the twelve is because he had been destined to play that role in God's plan of salvation. It is for this reason and no other reason that Judas betrayed Christ.

Some say when Judas ate the morsel of food when Christ dipped his bread was when Satan entered into Judas. If one is depicted a thief, it is obvious that the devil was already in him.

Christ knew Judas would betray Him as he knew that Peter would deny Him three times before the cock crowed. We need not theorize or opine further; nor do we need to try to analyze when Judas had Satan dictating his actions.

*****

Jesus, then, prays that his Father sanctifies his disciples, as He says, "Sanctify them through thy truth: thy word is truth." The word "sanctify" means to set apart for holy use. Jesus is asking his Father to bless his disciples and to make them productive in matters of holiness. He is praying to God for their purification. Jesus wants them to be spiritually blessed by his Father that they might be fruitful as they carry on with his work.

Jesus continues, "As thou hast sent me into the world, even so have I also sent them into the world." Jesus declares that He has commissioned his disciples to do his work. He has, in fact, by his declaration, ordained them, making them his messengers who will begin to build the church through which souls would be saved.

Jesus prays that they will be as one as He and his Father are one. His disciples were to be as one movement for Christ, preaching the gospel, praying for the sick, and doing all good works in the name of Jesus Christ who came to reconcile us to His Father, in heaven. Their message would be the same and they are to be fruitful as they declare Jesus Christ the Son of God who came to save all humanity from their sins.

His disciples are to be "one" as Jesus and his Father are one. Jesus states, "That they all may be one; as thou, Father, art in me, and I in thee, that they also may be one in us…" He adds, "That the world may believe that thou hast sent me."

The disciples are to preach salvation through Jesus as they declare that Jesus is the Son of God sent from heaven to offer His life for the sins of the world. The world, Jesus prays, must glorify Him because He is the Son of God, sent by his Father to offer everlasting life to those who believe in Him and keep his words.

In verse 24 of chapter 17 of John's Gospel, Jesus affirms His disciples' place with Him in heaven/paradise as He prays to the Father, saying, "Father, I will that they also, whom thou hast given me, *be with me where I am; that they may behold my glory*, which thou hast given me: for thou lovedst me before the foundation of the world."

This verse of scripture should leave no doubt in anyone's mind that Jesus' disciples would be with Him in heaven. Why? So they can be witness to His glorification as God would glorify Him.

After Jesus finished praying, He and His disciples left and crossed over the Cedron Brook in the Kedron Valley where there was an olive grove, and went forth into the Mount of Olives.

The Mount of Olives (also Mount Olivet, <u>Hebrew</u>: הר הזיתים, *Har HaZeitim*; Arabic: جبل الزيتون, الطور, *Jebel az-Zeitun*) is a mountain ridge in <u>East Jerusalem</u> with three peaks running from north to south. The highest, at-Tur, rises to 818 meters (2,683 ft.)

The Mount of Olives is frequently mentioned in the <u>New Testament</u> (<u>Matthew 21:1</u>; 26:30, etc.) as the route from Jerusalem to <u>Bethany</u> and the place where <u>Jesus</u> stood when He wept over Jerusalem.

Judas knew the place, also, because He had been there often with Jesus and the other disciples. And, he, Judas, having gone to the Temple and, with the Pharisees and chief priests, came with a band of men and officers carrying lanterns and torches, looking for Jesus.

And Jesus, because He knew all the things that were to happen; when He saw the group of men approaching, went forth and asked,   "Who are you looking for?"
Some cried out, "Jesus of Nazareth!"

*****

Before going further, let us look at just what took place before Judas and the others arrived. To do this, we must refer to the other gospels. We learned in the Gospel of St. John that Jesus, the night prior to his crucifixion, went to the Mount of Olives. As Jesus and his disciples entered the Mount of Olives they were in the place known as Gethsemane. According to the New Testament it was a place that Jesus and His disciples customarily visited, which allowed Judas to find Him on the night of His arrest.

Then cometh Jesus with them unto a place called Gethsemane, and said unto the disciples, "Sit here, while I go and pray yonder." Matthew 26:36

And they came to a place which was named

Gethsemane: and He said to his disciples, "Sit ye here, while I shall pray." Mark 14:32

The Gospel of St. Matthew 26:30 tells us that Jesus went to this garden called Gethsemane and took with Him Peter and the two sons of Zebedee, they being James and John, and was full of sorrow. Then He said unto them, "my soul is exceeding sorrowful, even unto death: tarry here, and watch with me." He, then, slowly moved away from His disciples, and then fell down to pray, "O my Father, if it be possible, let this <u>cup</u> pass from me; nevertheless, not as I will, but as thou will."

Jesus knew what was going to happen. He knew of the suffering He was going to have to endure. The cup He is referring to is the "cup of suffering" that we all must live with. It is a part of all of our lives.

Here we have the human element entering the story. Jesus is God, and in the scriptures we find evidence that, while on earth, He is a human being... a man, the same as me or any other man. As any man experiences sadness and sorrow, depression and fear, the unwillingness of pain if it can be avoided; so did Jesus.

The scriptures tell us He was very sorrowful and cried out to His Father, "Father, if it be possible let this cup pass from me." He doesn't want to suffer. No human being wants to suffer. And, that's exactly what Jesus was; a human being. But, Jesus, the God-man, knew exactly why He came to earth; He knew what His mission was and He knew it had to be accomplished. So, in spite of the pain He knew He was going to have to go through, and knowing that He, being the Son of God, somehow could have avoided it, He tells His Father, "Nevertheless, not as I will; not as I want or wish, but as you will; that is; let your will be done." He was telling his Father in heaven that He will

151

go through with the plan no matter what.

The question here is, why? Why is God willing to allow his Son, Jesus, to be subjected to the suffering that lay ahead and His violent death on the cross? And, why would Jesus be so willing to permit it to happen?

The Scriptures tell us that the Father, God, "gave" the life of His son for our sins. Read John 3:16, "For God so loved the world that he *gave* his only begotten son that whosoever believeth in him should not perish but have everlasting life." God "gave" the life of his Son for the remission of sins.

Some theologians say that God "offered" the life of His son for our sins. This is not true. Nothing in the scriptures indicates that God made the offer. He "gave" the life of his son. Jesus, and all those involved had to be part of God's plan that could restore man to his original state. That is to say; free of sin and existing in a paradise for all eternity.

Scripture tells us that God "gave" His son, Jesus, for our sins. Read 2 Corinthians 5:21, "For He hath <u>made</u> Him *to be* sin for us, who knew no sin; that we might be made the righteousness of God in Him." And, also, 1 John 4:10, "Herein is love, not that we loved God, but that <u>*he loved us, and sent his Son to be the propitiation for our sins.*</u>" This means that God sent Jesus, his son, to be an "atoning sacrifice"; thus, an "atoning sacrifice" meaning that He, Jesus, the propitiation for our sins is explained as such: the process by which a person removes obstacles for His reconciliation with God.

So, Jesus was sent by His Father for the purpose of reconciliation with the Father; a mission that had been planned long in advance by God, the Father, and Jesus, the Son, also God. The Book of Revelation 13:8 tells us that 'Jesus was slain from the foundations of the world.'

We who believe in God recognize that He is the author of all things. He is all knowing (omniscient), all powerful (omnipotent), and ever present (omnipresent) at all times. Nothing is unclear to Him and nothing comes as a surprise. He, obviously, has the complete "blueprint" concerning all of us, and that included Jesus, His son, our Redeemer.

Because of his tremendous love for all of us, did He want us to be reconciled to himself? So, He, God, made a plan that would involve the only one perfect enough to be the price for our sins. And, that perfect entity was Jesus, God. (God Incarnate... God become man for the atonement of all sins). Again, God is three individual entities; God, the Father, Jesus, the Son, and the Holy Spirit).

And, because it was known that Jesus would be slain from the foundations of the world, the prophets of old foretold of the event. Had Jesus not followed through with the "plan" the prophecies could not have been fulfilled.

Did Jesus give His life willingly? Of course He did. John 10:18 tells us that Jesus, indeed, gave His life willingly. He says, "No man takes it from me (Jesus is talking about his life), but I lay it down of myself. I have power to lay it down, and I have power to take it again. This commandment have I received of my Father."

So, Jesus did give his life willingly even though He had the power to keep it. But, why did He ask the Father to "remove the cup" from Him if it was possible? Because, being a man, He knew He would have to go through a tremendous amount of suffering and then die a most horrible death! No man wants to go through such an experience. But, also, being God, He immediately told His Father, "let it be your will be done and not as I will it" (paraphrased).

Jesus could have called upon legions of angels to hurry

to his defense to put an end to the impending suffering and death, but, of course, this would be the thoughts He would have had if he'd been thinking as a man would think. He had already told Peter as stated in the Gospel of St. Matthew 26: 53-54, "Thinkest thou that I cannot now pray to my Father, and he shall presently give me more than twelve legions of angels?" He adds, "But how then shall the scriptures be fulfilled, that thus it must be?" The Old Testament was filled with prophesies of Jesus, and how He would be persecuted and die. If He had stopped it, the prophecies would not have been fulfilled. Jesus would never let this happen.

God never offered his son's life to be the payment for our sins. He gave his son's life because of his tremendous love for us. And Jesus willingly gave His own life; in other words, He had to agree to go along with God's plan of salvation for the whole world. So, the answer to our question as to why God gave His son and why Jesus willing made the sacrifice was simply because of God's love for us.

*****

The Gospel of St. John does not record what was known as the Transfiguration. In the Synoptic Gospels, (Matthew 17:1-9, Mark 9:2-8, Luke 9:28-36) the account of the transfiguration happens towards the middle of the narrative. It is a key episode and almost immediately follows another important element, the *Confession of Peter*: "you are the Christ". The Transfiguration narrative acts as a further revelation of the identity of Jesus as the Son of God to some of His disciples.

In the Gospels, Jesus takes Peter, James, son of Zebedee and John the Apostle with Him and goes up to a mountain, which is not named. Once on the mountain, Matthew (17:2) states that Jesus "was transfigured before them; His face shining as the sun, and His garments became white as the light." At that point the prophets Elijah and Moses appear and Jesus begins to talk to them.[1] Luke is specific in describing Jesus in a state of glory, with Luke 9:32 referring to "they saw His glory."

Just as Elijah and Moses begin to depart from the scene, Peter begins to ask Jesus if the disciples should make three tents, one for Jesus and the two prophets. This is at times interpreted as Peter's attempt to keep the prophets there longer. But before Peter can finish a bright cloud appears, and a voice from the cloud states, "This is my beloved Son, with whom I am well pleased; listen to him". The disciples then fall to the ground in fear, but Jesus approaches and touches them, telling them not to be afraid. When the disciples look up, they no longer see Elijah or Moses.

When Jesus and the three apostles are going back down the mountain, Jesus tells them to not to tell anyone "the things they had seen" until the "Son of Man" has risen from the dead. The apostles are described as questioning among themselves as to what Jesus meant by "risen from the dead".

In addition to the principal account given in the Synoptic Gospels; in 2 Peter 1:16-18, Apostle Peter describes himself as an eyewitness "of His sovereign majesty." The Gospel of John may also briefly allude to the same episode in John: 1-14.

Elsewhere in the New Testament, Apostle Paul's reference in 2 Corinthians 3:18 to the "transformation of believers" via "beholding as in a mirror the glory of the Lord" became the theological basis for considering the Transfiguration as the basis for processes which lead the faithful to the knowledge of God.

__Christian theology__ assigns a great deal of significance to the Transfiguration, based on multiple elements of the narrative. In Christian teachings, the Transfiguration is a pivotal moment, and the setting on the mountain is presented as the point where human nature meets God: the meeting place for the temporal and the eternal, with Jesus himself as the connecting point, acting as the bridge between heaven and earth.

The Transfiguration not only supports the identity of Jesus as the __Son of God__ (as in his __Baptism__), but the statement "listen to Him", identifies Him as the messenger and mouth-piece of God. The significance of this identification is enhanced by the presence of Elijah and Moses, for it indicates to the apostles that Jesus is the voice of God "par excellence", and instead of Elijah or Moses, He should be listened to, surpassing the laws of Moses by virtue of His filial relationship with God.

— __2 Peter 1:16-18__, echoes the same message. At the Transfiguration God assigns to Jesus a special "honor and glory" and it is the turning point at which God exalts Jesus above all other powers in creation, and positions Him as ruler and judge.

The Transfiguration also echoes the teaching by Jesus (as in __Matthew 22:32__) that God is not "the God of the dead, but of the living". Although Moses and Elijah had died centuries before, they could live in the presence of the Son of God, implying that the same return to life can apply to all who face death.[18]

*****

Chapter XV

Jesus Is Arrested
Jesus on Trial
Peter Denies Christ

When the band of men, accompanied by Judas, approached Jesus inquiring of Him, Jesus told them, "I am he." When they heard the Lord's reply, they fell backward, fell to the ground and said nothing. Jesus asked them again, "Whom do you seek?"

Jesus said, "I have told you that I am he." Jesus knew why they had come and told them, "If you have come for me; let these others go" (referring to His disciples). Peter noted the belligerent attitude of those who had come for Jesus and immediately drew his sword and cut off the ear of the high priests' servant, Malchus.

*****

In the scripture above we are told that Peter had been carrying a sword. The question most people ask is, "If Jesus was always preaching peace and telling the crowds to turn the other cheek, why did Peter have a sword and why did Jesus permit him to carry one?"

Most theologians will tell us that in those days one had to protect himself. We are told that there were many thieves and bandits roaming the country sides and it was necessary for everyone to protect themselves. As a matter of fact, if you read the Gospel of St. Luke 22:36, Jesus is telling His listeners to go and buy a sword if they don't have one. On the one hand, Jesus is telling His disciples to love each other, turn the other cheek, and love their enemies, while on the other hand He is telling them to sell their goods and buy a sword.

Many theologians tell us that even though Jesus

instructed His disciples to buy a sword; He did not want them to use their swords. I, for one, cannot picture the disciples' sword fighting with those who opposed them. To me, the followers of Jesus Christ, having swords, and being ready to use them to fight, doesn't make any sense at all. Nevertheless, we are told that Jesus told them to go buy a sword. Peter obviously did as Jesus instructed and, not only was he prepared to use it; he did.

Was Jesus wrong in telling his disciples to sell what they had and buy a sword? I don't know. Yet, we must ask ourselves this question: "is it wrong for anyone to want to protect ones' self and those he loves?" In the Old Testament we read of many incidents where those serving God used the sword. In this case when the band of men came after Jesus, Peter, having the sword immediately took action to defend his master. He swung his sword violently and cut off the ear of the high priests' servant. Jesus, we are told, later restored it (Read the incident in its entirety in Luke 26: 27-56).

Jesus quickly told Peter to put away his sword. He didn't want Peter, or anyone else to defend Him or interfere, for He says, "The cup that my Father gave me; shall I not drink it?"

Christ didn't tell Peter to put up his sword because he (Peter) was merely trying to defend Him; He was insisting to Peter that he should not interfere with what was going on because He had to "drink" of the cup his Father gave Him. Nothing should interfere with the "plan". Jesus had to drink from the cup. He had to suffer, and He had to die on the cross. Only when this was accomplished would His mission be completed.

Though it is not recorded in scripture, it is obvious that most, if not all of Jesus' disciples carried swords. It could be that they carried the swords as they traveled to "deter" those who would have believed that Jesus and those who followed Him would be a "soft touch." In modern days, it had been suggested by many that the best way to avoid conflict is to have, or show, a strong defense. I will say no more about the sword.

After the incident with Peter and Malchus' ear, the high priests and the officers took hold of Jesus and bound Him (this was after we are told in the synoptic gospels that Judas identified his master by kissing Him). They quickly brought Jesus to Annas who was the father-in-law to Caiaphas, the High Priest that year.

Annas, though not the high priest, was the most influential. Annas had been High Priest (AD 6-15) and was still head of the ruling High Priestly family. These were Sadducees whose policy was to submit to Roman rule but manipulate it to get their own way wherever possible.

They held office by Roman appointment as puppet rulers, but sometimes it was not clear who was pulling the strings. Annas was father-in-law to Caiaphas and the real power was shared between them. The family profited from the trade in the temple courtyard; so Jesus made enemies of them by driving the traders out. The first time He did this (John 2) made Him a public figure. The crowd supported Him, and the fact that He could so defy the authorities, shows how popular and influential He was.

Annas was a staunch enemy of Jesus and wanted Jesus' death. He planned Jesus' death cautiously with the help of his son-in-law Caiaphas. He was sagacious and clever who knew how to manipulate the Romans and the Sanhedrin in order to stay in power.

Annas, after briefly questioning Jesus, had Him brought to his son-in-law Caiaphas. It was he who had already counseled the Jews that, "it was expedient that one man should die for the people" (See St. John 11:50).

$$*****$$

(Here we will leave the Gospel of St. John and pick up at Chapter 26 in the Gospel of St. Matthew and Jesus is on trial before Caiaphas and the Sanhedrin).

Those who had taken Jesus led Him away to <u>Caiaphas</u> the high priest, where the scribes and the <u>elders</u> were gathered together. <u>Peter</u> followed Him from a distance, to the court of the high priest, and entered in and sat with the officers, to see the end.

Now the chief priests, the <u>elders</u>, and the whole council sought false testimony against Jesus, that they might put Him to death; and they found none. Even though many false witnesses came forward, they found none. But at last two false witnesses came forward, and said, "This man said, 'I am able to destroy the <u>temple</u> of God, and to build it in three days.'"

The high priest stood up, and said to Him, "Have you no answer? What is this that these <u>testify</u> against you?" But Jesus held His peace. The high priest answered Him, "I adjure you by the living God, that you tell us whether you are the <u>Christ</u>, the Son of God."

Jesus said to him, "You have said it. Nevertheless, I tell you, after this you will see the Son of Man sitting at the right hand of Power, and coming on the clouds of the sky."

Then the high priest tore his clothing, saying, "He has spoken blasphemy! Why do we need any more witnesses? <u>Behold</u>, now you have heard His blasphemy. What do you think?"

They answered, "He is worthy of death!" Then they spit in His face and beat Him with their fists, and some slapped

Him, saying, "Prophesy to us you <u>Christ</u>! Who hit you?"

(Wikipedia, the free encyclopedia, examines the trial of Jesus Christ by the Sanhedrin and it is herein stated):

<u>From Wikipedia, the free encyclopedia</u>

The Sanhedrin trial of Jesus refers to the <u>Canonical Gospel</u> accounts of the trial of <u>Jesus</u> before the Jewish Council, or <u>Sanhedrin</u>, following <u>his arrest</u> and prior to his trial before <u>Pontius Pilate</u>. It is an event reported by all four Canonical gospels of the <u>Bible</u>, although <u>John's Gospel</u> does not explicitly mention the Sanhedrin in this context.

The Gospels report that after <u>Jesus</u> and His followers celebrated <u>Passover</u> as their <u>Last Supper</u>, Jesus was betrayed by His <u>apostle</u> <u>Judas Iscariot</u>, and <u>arrested</u> in the <u>Garden of Gethsemane</u>. Jesus was then taken to the high priest's house where He was mocked and beaten. Jesus is generally quiet, does not mount a defense, and rarely responds to the accusations, but is condemned by the Jewish authorities when He will not deny that He is the <u>Son of God</u>. The Jewish leaders then take Jesus to <u>Pontius Pilate</u>, the governor of <u>Roman Judaea,</u> and ask him to kill Jesus for claiming to be the <u>King of the Jews</u>.

The trial most probably took place informally on Thursday night and then again formally on Friday morning (see the article on <u>Crucifixion of Jesus</u> for a discussion on the exact date of <u>Good Friday</u>, which in recent years has been estimated as AD 33, by different groups of scientists).

*****

In the narrative of the <u>Canonical Gospels</u> after the <u>betrayal and arrest</u> of Jesus, He is taken to the <u>Sanhedrin</u>, a Jewish judicial body. From a historical perspective, in the era in which the narrative is set, this body was an <u>ad hoc</u> gathering, rather than a fixed court.

In the four canonical gospels Jesus is tried and condemned by the Sanhedrin, mocked and beaten and is condemned for making the claim of being the <u>Son of God</u>. Although the Gospel accounts vary with respect to various details, they agree on the general character and overall structure of the trials of Jesus.

In all four Gospel accounts the trial of Jesus before the priests and scribes is interweaved with the <u>Denial of Peter</u> narrative, where <u>Apostle Peter</u> who has followed Jesus denies knowing Him three times. <u>Luke 22:61</u> states that as Jesus was bound and standing at the priest's house Peter was in the courtyard. Jesus "turned and looked straight at him", and Peter remembered the words Jesus had spoken to him: "Before the rooster crows today, you will disown me three times."

In the Gospel accounts Jesus speaks very little, and gives very infrequent and indirect answers to the questions of the priests, prompting an officer to slap Him. In <u>Matthew 26:62</u> the lack of response from Jesus prompts the high priest to ask Him: "Answerest thou nothing?" In the Gospel accounts the men that hold Jesus at the high priest's house mock, blindfold, insult and beat Him, at times slapping Him and asking Him to guess who had hit Him that time.

<u>Mark 14:55-59</u> states that the chief priests had sought witness against Jesus to put Him to death but did not find any, so they arranged false witness against Him, but their witness did not agree together. <u>Mark 14:61</u> states that the high priest then asked Jesus: "Art thou the <u>Christ</u>, the Son of the Blessed? And Jesus said, "I am" at which point the high priest tore his own robe in anger and accused Jesus of

blasphemy.

In <u>Matthew 26:63</u> the high priest asks: "tell us whether you are the Christ, the Son of God." Jesus responds "You have said it" prompting the priest to tear his own robe.

In <u>Luke 22:67</u> Jesus is asked: "If thou art the Christ, tell us. But He said unto them, "If I tell you, ye will not believe". But, in <u>22:70</u> when asked: "Are you then the Son of God?" Jesus answers: "You say that I am" affirming the title <u>Son of God</u>. At that point the priests say: "What further need have we of witness? For we ourselves have heard from His own mouth" and decide to condemn Jesus.

While Jesus was before the Sanhedrin, on trial, Peter was in the outer court waiting for the outcome. While he waited, the Gospel of John informs us that there was a damsel who "kept the door" and when she saw Peter, she asked him, "Are you not one of Jesus' disciples?"

Peter, quickly, replied, "I am not!"

It was cold that night and the officers and servants made a coal fire and gathered around it to keep warm. Peter was also cold and stood with them beside the fire. While Peter stood warming himself, some asked him, "Aren't you one of Jesus' disciples?"

Peter said, "I am not!" This was the second time Peter denied even knowing Jesus.

*****

One of the servants of the high priest, being his kinsman whose ear Peter cut off, asked, "Did not I see you in the garden with Him?" Peter then denied again: and immediately the cock crowed.

*****

However, even though the Sanhedrin had decided to, and did, condemn Jesus to death, they could not. They insisted to Pilate that they (the Sanhedrin) had not the authority to put a man to death. This, of course was not true.

Any Jewish scholar will attest that capital punishment was not only authorized by Jewish law but also practiced by the Sanhedrin in the time of Jesus. In fact, the Acts of the Apostles tells us Stephen, something of an early church deacon, was put to death by stoning on order of the Sanhedrin. Acts 7:54-60. What possible reason can there be for the Sanhedrin to tell Pilate that they lack authority to put Jesus to death? The only logical answer is if Jesus was a Roman citizen. In such a case, only the Romans could lawfully carry out a death sentence. Jesus would have been a Roman citizen by birth if His father held Roman citizenship.

The records might have indicated that the father of Joseph, Jesus' earthly father, was, or could have been of Roman birth and held Roman citizenship. No one really knows.

(There is a great deal of controversy among noted theologians as to who was Joseph's father. Perhaps his father's name was Heli but no one can be absolutely sure).

*****

It was over as far as the Sanhedrin was concerned. They had judged Jesus and, according to them, Jesus was to die. He had been accused of blasphemy because Jesus had declared himself the Christ, the Son of God.

The Jewish leaders then took Jesus to <u>Pontius Pilate</u>, the governor of <u>Roman Judaea</u> and asked him to kill Jesus for claiming to be the <u>King of the Jews</u>.

(Some of the information below concerning the trial of Jesus Christ is taken from Wikipedia, the free encyclopedia for two reasons. The first reason is; I didn't feel compelled to bounce around, back and forth from gospel to gospel, etc. with the various details only because my theological studies over the years, when compared to Wikipedia information; the information as presented by Wikipedia, in my own mind, had to be the way the trial of Jesus had been conducted).

*****

In the four Canonical Gospels, Jesus is tried and condemned by the Sanhedrin, mocked and beaten and is condemned for making the claim of being the <u>Son of God</u>. Although the Gospel accounts vary with respect to various details, they agree on the general character and overall structure of the trials of Jesus.

*****

<u>Matthew 26:57</u> states that Jesus was taken to the house of <u>Caiaphas</u> the high priest, where the scribes and the elders were gathered together and in <u>Matthew 27:1</u> adds that the next morning the priests held another meeting. <u>Mark 14:53</u> states that Jesus was taken that night "to the high priest" (without naming the priest) where all the chief priests and the elders gathered, and in <u>Mark 15:1</u> it adds that another consultation was held among the priests the next morning. <u>Luke 22:54</u> states that Jesus was taken to "the high priest's house" (without naming the priest) where He was mocked and beaten that night and in <u>22:66</u> it adds that "as soon as it was day", the chief priests and scribes gathered together and led Jesus away into their council.

In <u>John 18:12-14</u>, however, Jesus is first taken to <u>Annas</u>, the father-in-law of Caiaphas, who was the current <u>high priest</u> at that time. Annas is believed to have been the former high priest and it appears that Caiaphas sought Annas' confirmation of Caiaphas' actions. In <u>18:24</u> Jesus is sent from Annas to Caiaphas, the high priest, and <u>18:28</u> states that in the morning, Jesus was led from Caiaphas to Pontius Pilate in the Praetorian (the location).

In all four Gospel accounts the trial of Jesus before the priests and scribes is interleaved with the <u>Denial of Peter</u> narrative, where <u>Apostle Peter</u> who has followed Jesus denies knowing him three times. <u>Luke 22:61</u> states that as Jesus was bound and standing at the priest's house Peter was in the courtyard. Jesus "turned and looked straight at Him", and Peter remembered the words Jesus had spoken to him: "Before the rooster crows today, you will disown me three times."

In the Gospel accounts Jesus speaks very little, and gives very infrequent and indirect answers to the questions of the priests, prompting an officer to slap Him. In <u>Matthew 26:62</u> the lack of response from Jesus prompts the high priest to ask Him: "Answerest thou nothing?" In the Gospel accounts the men that hold Jesus at the high priest's house mock, blindfold, insult, and beat Him, at times slapping Him and asking Him to guess who had hit Him that time.

<u>Mark 14:55-59</u> states that the chief priests had sought witness against Jesus to put Him to death but did not find any, so they arranged false witness against Him, but their witnesses did not agree together. <u>Mark 14:61</u> states that the high priest then asked Jesus: "Art thou the <u>Christ</u>, the Son of the Blessed? And Jesus said, I am" at which point the high priest tore his own robe in anger and accused Jesus of blasphemy. In <u>Matthew 26:63</u> the high priest asks: "tell us whether you are the Christ, the Son of God." Jesus responds "You have said it", prompting the priest to tear his own robe.

In <u>Luke 22:67</u> Jesus is asked: "If thou art the Christ, tell us. But he said unto them, "If I tell you, ye will not believe". But, in 22:70 when asked: "Are you then the Son of God?" Jesus answers: "You say that I am" affirming the title Son of God.[115] At that point the priests say: "What further need have we of witness; for we ourselves have heard from His own mouth" and decide to condemn Jesus.

Thereafter in Pilate's Court the Jewish elders ask Pontius Pilate to judge and condemn Jesus – accusing Him of claiming to be the King of the Jews.

*****

Nothing above mentions that Pontius Pilate sent Jesus to King Herod. When Pilate heard that Jesus was a Galilean, he sent Jesus to King Herod who was in Jerusalem at the time. This is recorded in the Gospel of St. Luke Chapter 23.

"This man comes under King Herod's jurisdiction!" he might have told the Jewish leaders. "Bring Him to King Herod! He will deal with Him!"

And so they did. And when Herod saw Jesus he was very glad because he had heard about the man and the many miracles He performed. King Herod was, himself, anxious to question Jesus and had hoped Jesus would perform a miracle or two for him.

But, Jesus remained silent and would do nothing requested of Him by the king. Herod's officers mocked Jesus and ridiculed Him. They, then, placed upon Him a gorgeous robe that was fit for a king. When they were through mocking Jesus they sent Him back to Pilate.

*****

Here, I must tell you some things about Pontius Pilate and his wife. Pontius Pilate's wife's name is not mentioned at all in any of the gospels in the New Testament. Nevertheless, theologians have, after much research concluded to call her Procia. According to the Gospel of St.

Matthew 27:19, she sent a message to her husband asking him not to condemn Jesus. She told her husband to have nothing to do with that innocent man. She states further, "In a dream last night, I suffered much on account of Him."

In the Eastern Orthodox Church and in the Ethiopian Orthodox Church she is a saint. She is referred to, also, as St. Procula. She might, also, been called Claudia as indicated in the Epistle Timothy 4:21 where we read, "Eubulus, Pudens, Linus and Claudia send their greetings, and so do all the other Christians." We cannot be sure that Paul is referring to Pontius Pilate's wife.

Of course, we know through scripture that Pilate did not heed his wife's warning to not condemn Jesus. The 2nd century historian, Origen, in his Homilies on Matthew suggests that she became a Christian, or at least that God sent her the dream mentioned by Matthew so that she would become one. Quite a few theologians felt the same as did Origen regarding Pilate's wife and that she did become a Christian.

However, many other theologians felt otherwise. Some of them believed that Pilate's wife's dream was a product of the devil. They believe that the dream was an attempt to discourage the salvation that would be the result of Jesus' death.

A letter, purportedly written in Latin by Pilate's wife from "a little Gallic mountain town" several years after Pilate left <u>Jerusalem</u>, was first published in English by *Pictorial Review Magazine* in April 1929. The English version of the letter was provided by writer Catherine Van Dyke and it states that Pilate's wife successfully sought Jesus' aid to heal the crippled foot of her son Pilo.

Pontius Pilate was the fifth prefect of the Roman

Province of Judea. He is best known as the judge at the trial of Jesus and the person who ordered Christ be crucified. It is obvious that a prefect was Rome's highest official in any one of Rome's provinces which included Judea. The prefect had to be the official who passed on laws from Rome to the people, saw to the collection of taxes, and, in essence, acted as judge when necessary. Pontius Pilate was the Prefect in Judea for 10 years. According to Josephus, the historian who authored "Jewish Antiquities", Pilate was ordered back to Rome after harshly suppressing a <u>Samaritan</u> uprising, arriving just after Tiberius' death in AD 36. He was replaced by <u>Marcellus</u>.

In all four of the gospels, Pilate appears to be in association with the Jewish leaders for the crucifixion of Jesus, yet, scripture tells us that he was very reluctant to order the death of Christ. In the Gospel of St. Matthew he washes his hands to indicate that he was not responsible for the death of Jesus and reluctantly sends him to His death. In the Gospel of St. Mark, Jesus is depicted as completely innocent of plotting against the Roman Empire and, again, Pilate is depicted as extremely reluctant to condemn Jesus to death. Pilate, in St. Mark, blames the Jewish priestly hierarchy for Jesus' death and he washes his hands as in St. Matthew; not of Jesus, but of the Sadducees and of any association with their actions. In St. Luke, Pilate not only agrees that Jesus did not conspire against Rome, but <u>Herod Antipas</u>, the Tetrarch of <u>Galilee</u>, also finds nothing treasonable in Jesus' actions. Scholars have long debated how to interpret Pilate's portrayal in the sources.

Some <u>Biblical scholars</u> have argued that the Gospel accounts are not historically accurate with some believing Pilate was a mythical character. The discovery of the Pilate

Stone in 1961 confirmed his historicity as a Prefect and added to the <u>credence of the Gospel accounts.</u>

(<u>Some</u> data provided by Wikipedia, the free encyclopedia).

*****

(More on Prefect/Procurator Duties and Responsibilities)

Their primary function was military but they were responsible for the collection of imperial taxes. They had limited judicial functions. Others in civil administration were responsible to see that the local government functioned smoothly. In the course of performing his duties, Pilate traveled throughout the province, especially to Jerusalem, from his home which was in Caesarea.

During the <u>Passover</u>, a festival of deep national as well as religious significance for the Jews, Pilate, as governor or prefect, would have been expected to be in Jerusalem to keep order. He would not ordinarily be visible to the throngs of worshippers because of the Jewish people's deep sensitivity to their status as a Roman province.

Equestrians such as Pilate could command legionary forces but only small ones, and so in military situations, he would have to yield to his superior, the legate of Syria, who would descend into Palestine with his legions as necessary. As governor of Judaea, Pilate would have small auxiliary forces of locally recruited soldiers stationed regularly in Caesarea and Jerusalem, such as the <u>Antonia Fortress</u>, and temporarily anywhere else that might require a military presence. The total number of soldiers at Pilate's disposal numbered in the range of 3000.

Ancient Jewish writers, Philo and Josephus, describe some of the other events and incidents that took place during Pilate's tenure. Both Josephus and Philo reported that Pilate repeatedly caused near-insurrections among the Jews because of his insensitivity to Jewish customs.

In describing Pilate's personality, Philo writes that Pilate had "vindictiveness and a furious temper," and was "naturally inflexible, a blend of self-will and relentlessness." He writes that Pilate feared a delegation that the Jews might send to Tiberius protesting the gold-coated shields, because "if they actually sent an embassy they would also expose the rest of his conduct as governor by stating in full the briberies, the insults, the robberies, the outrages and wanton injuries, the executions without trial constantly repeated, the ceaseless and supremely grievous cruelty."

*****

Pilate's term as prefect of Judaea ended after an incident recounted by Josephus. A large group of Samaritans had been persuaded by an unnamed man to go to Mount Gerizim in order to see sacred artifacts allegedly buried by Moses. But at a village named Tirathana, before the crowd could ascend the mountain, Pilate sent in "a detachment of cavalry and heavy-armed infantry, who in an encounter with the first comers in the village slew some in a pitched battle and put the others to flight. Many prisoners were taken, of whom Pilate put to death the principal leaders and those who were most influential." The Samaritans then complained to Vitellius, Roman governor of Syria, who sent Pilate to Rome to explain his actions regarding this incident to Tiberius. However, by the time Pilate got to Rome, Tiberius had died. *(Again, you can learn much about Pontius Pilate by visiting www.wikipedia.org, the free encyclopedia. Some of the information above was from this source).

Chapter XVI

Jesus Is Scourged and Beaten
Pilate Questions Jesus and Condemns Him
Jesus is put to Death

According to the Gospel of St. John, Pilate had Jesus brought into the hall of justice again and questioned Him, asking "Are you the King of the Jews?"

Jesus replied "Do you say this thing of yourself or did others tell you this?"

Pilate answered angrily, "Am I a Jew?" He looked away as if frustrated, and then turned again to face Jesus. "Your own nation and the chief priests delivered you to me! What have you done?"

Jesus answered, slowly and deliberately, saying "My kingdom is not of this world; if it were my servants would fight that I might be free."

"Are you a king, then?" Pilate demanded an answer.

Jesus, his head bowed, said "You say that I am a king. For this reason was I born, and for this cause I came into the world that I should be a witness to the truth. Everyone who understands truth hears my voice."

Pilate, a bit confused, after scratching his head, asks Jesus, "What is truth?"

Jesus stood silent as if by just standing there he was making a statement. Jesus had already told Pilate that He was a witness unto the truth and "everyone who understands truth hears my voice." What is truth? Jesus is truth! The Jews and those who heard Him speak who know the scriptures and were open to the truth, came to understand that He was truth. He spoke of forgiving, and loving each other. He showed compassion and mercy that could come only from a loving and caring God. He referred all too often to the prophets of the Old Testament concerning the things He taught. He knew that the Jews were following what Moses taught and the laws he passed down. Moses' law was truth and Jesus never disputed them when teaching the Jews.

In the Gospel of St. Matthew, KJV, 5:17-19 Jesus made it clear to those who heard Him. He said, "Think not that I am come to destroy the law, or the prophets: I am not come to destroy, but to fulfill. For verily I say unto you, "Till heaven and earth pass, one jot or one title shall in no wise pass from the law, till all be fulfilled. Whosoever therefore shall break one of these least commandments, and shall teach men so, he shall be called the least in the kingdom of heaven: but whosoever shall do and teach *them*, the same shall be called great in the kingdom of heaven."

Jesus, the Son of God, spoke the truth concerning His Father and those who heard Him knew this. When Pilate asked Jesus, "what is truth?" Jesus stood silent because, by His silence, He was telling Pilate and the world that _He_ is truth. Pilate, not being a Jew, had never heard Jesus speak and nor had he been a witness to the miracles He performed so he could not know what Jesus was referring to. Pilate, it was obvious, saw before him a troubled, confused, day dreamer; a person, perhaps, seeking notoriety, or, one who might have been a "mental case."

When Pilate went out again among the Jews he announced to them, "I find no fault in this man!"

Of course, the chief priests and the Sadducees who were there to do all they could to have Jesus condemned were upset with Pilate's findings and became furious.

"But, you have a custom!" Pilate shouted. "In honor of your Feast of the Passover I will release unto you one of our prisoners."

*****

Three gospels state that there was a custom at Passover during which the Roman governor would release a prisoner of the crowd's choice: Mark 15:6; Matthew 27:15; and John 18:39. Later copies of Luke contain a corresponding verse (Luke 23:17), though it is not present in the earliest manuscripts, and may be a later gloss to bring Luke into conformity.

No custom of releasing prisoners in Jerusalem is recorded in any *historical* document other than the gospels. An Ancient Roman celebration called <u>Lectisternium</u> involved feasting and sometimes included a temporary removal of the chains from all prisoners. However, J. Blinzler associates Barabbas' release with a passage in the Mishna Peshahim 8, 6 which says that the Passover lamb may be offered 'for one whom they have promised to bring out of prison' (J. Blinzler, The Trial of Jesus, 1959, pp218ff).

Yet, there is no real evidence in any historical documents, other than the gospels, that there is a custom that a prisoner could be released in celebration of any of the Jewish feasts. And, it is very unlikely that any governor/procurator would ever release a prisoner for any reason. The Gospel of St. John tells us that Barabbas was a robber. But, he was also an insurrectionist and a murderer.

But, as per the gospels, the custom was such that a prisoner would be released by popular acclaim. Barabbas, a zealot, was a prisoner at the time. And according to the gospels, and the customs, either Jesus would be released or, the violent criminal, Barabbas. The penalty for Barabbas' crime was death by <u>crucifixion</u>.

Though the Gospels tell us that Barabbas was a robber and a murderer, they do tell us he was a rebel, an insurrectionist, a robber _and_ a murderer; his victims were more than likely Roman soldiers.

There are absolutely no biblical records, or historic records, that would tell us where Barabbas was born, when he was born, and when he died. We do know that he was a character who fit in perfectly at the time.

The chief priests and Sadducees knew Barabbas was in prison at the time and that, as per the custom described above, the choice would be Jesus or Barabbas. _One_ was to be released by popular acclaim. This meant that those who hollered and screamed the loudest would see their choice go free.

The chief priests and Sadducees, it appeared, incited the crowd, most of who were paid and granted favors if they would cry out in favor of Barabbas. Besides, Barabbas was a rebel and fiercely opposed the Romans who oppressed them.

And, it is obvious that the choice offered came about early in the morning when most people who knew and loved Jesus were still asleep. The chief priests and Sadducees had only to call out the rabble and trouble makers, offer them whatever it was they offered, and they could, easily, accomplish the condemnation of Jesus.

(You can learn more about Barabbas by visiting Wikipedia, the free encyclopedia on line).

*****

So, the choice was offered and the crowd cried out, "Give us Barabbas! Give us Barabbas!"

But what of Jesus of Nazareth? "In Him I find no fault! What shall I do with Him?" Pilate queried.

And they cried out loud, saying "Crucify Him! Let Him be crucified!"

The chief priests and Sadducees also cried out, "Crucify

Him!"

Than Pilate said, as if exasperated and frustrated, "Behold the man!"

Before Pilate presented Jesus to make his final plea on behalf of an innocent man, he ordered that Jesus be scourged. That is to say; He was violently whipped, spat upon, and mocked. The soldiers crowned Jesus with a crown of thorns and placed upon Him a purple robe. After doing this, the soldiers further attempted to humiliate Christ by shouting, "Hail! King of the Jews!" And, several of them slapped Jesus on His face as blood streamed down His forehead and onto His face.

As Jesus stood before the crowd, they continued to shout out, "Crucify Him! Crucify Him!"

Again, Pilate withdrew to the hall of justice and had Jesus brought before him. "Who are you?" Pilate asked Jesus, softly. "Where did you come from"?

Jesus did not respond to Pilate's questions.

"Why do you not answer me?" Pilate asked. "Don't you know that I have the power to have you crucified or have you released?"

Jesus responded quickly, saying, "You would have no power at all against me had it not been given you from above. Therefore, he that delivered me to you has the greater sin."

Once again before the crowd, Pilate, it seems, made further attempts to save Jesus, telling them, "I find no fault in Him!"

"This man made himself the Son of God," they cried out. Then, they added, "We have a law, and by that law He must die! If you let this man go free, you are not Caesar's friend! Whoever makes himself a king speaks against Caesar."

When Pilate therefore heard that saying, he brought Jesus forth, and sat down in the judgment seat in a place that is called the Pavement, but in the Hebrew, Gabbatha. And it was the preparation of the Passover, and about the sixth hour: and he said unto the Jews, "Behold your King!"

But the crowd cried out, "Away with Him, away with Him, crucify Him!"

Pilate asked them, "Shall I crucify your King?"

And, the chief priest answered, "We have no king but Caesar."

Pontius Pilate could not argue further in Jesus' behalf. To state that there was a king other than Caesar anywhere Caesar ruled was, of course, certain death. In other words, Jesus could not be King of the Jews because Caesar is the King. You dare not declare anyone King in Judea and live to tell about it. So, Jesus had to die and it was the Jews who made it happen. And, the Gospel of St. John tells us; they took Jesus and led him away!

*****

Here we will examine what the other gospels have to say about the Crucifixion of Jesus Christ. Jesus Christ, the man we who are Christians believe is the Son of God and Messiah, was arrested, tried, and sentenced by Pontius Pilate to be crucified on a cross.

Jesus' crucifixion is described in all four canonical gospels, attested to by other contemporary sources, and regarded as a historical event. Christians believe Jesus' suffering was foretold in Hebrew scripture such as in Psalm 22 and Isaiah's songs of the suffering servant. According to the New Testament, Jesus was arrested in Gethsemane following the Last Supper with the twelve Apostles, and forced to stand trial before the Sanhedrin, Pontius Pilate, and <u>Herod Antipas</u>, before being handed over for crucifixion. After being <u>flogged</u>, Jesus was mocked by Roman soldiers as the "<u>King of the Jews</u>", clothed in a purple robe, crowned with thorns, beaten and spat on. Jesus then had to make His way to the <u>place of His crucifixion</u>.

Once at <u>Golgotha</u>, Jesus was offered wine mixed with gall to drink. Matthew and Mark's Gospels record that He refused this. He was then crucified and hung between two convicted thieves. According to Mark's Gospel, He endured the torment of crucifixion for some six hours from the third hour, at approximately 9 am until His death at the ninth hour, corresponding to about 3 pm. The soldiers affixed a sign above His head stating "Jesus of Nazareth, King of the Jews" in <u>three languages</u>, divided His garments, and cast lots for His seamless robe. The Roman soldiers did not break Jesus' legs, as they did to the other two men crucified (breaking the legs hastened the crucifixion process), as Jesus was dead already. Each gospel has its own account of Jesus' last words, <u>seven statements</u> altogether. In the <u>Synoptic Gospels</u>, Matthew, Mark, and Luke, various <u>supernatural events</u> accompany the crucifixion, including <u>darkness</u>, an earthquake, and (in Matthew) the resurrection of saints

Following Jesus' death, His body was removed from the cross by <u>Joseph of Arimathea</u> and buried in a <u>rock-hewn tomb</u>, with <u>Nicodemus</u> assisting. According to Christian

tradition, Jesus then <u>rose from the dead</u> three days later.

Jesus was made to carry His own cross to the place of crucifixion which was called Golgotha (Place of a skull). By the time He began his trek to Golgotha, His physical condition had to be critical. Having had no food, water, and sleep He had to be weak and possibly in shock. According to ancient documents and noted historians, those who were apt to be crucified were scourged, denied water, and deprived of sleep prior to the event so as to shorten the time it would take for them to die while on the cross.

There can be no doubt that up to the Last Supper and prior to Jesus' arrest and trial His physical condition was probably quite good. Even with all the traveling in Jerusalem and the surrounding country side on foot, preaching, teaching, and praying for the sick... though He had to have been consistently in a "worn out" condition. There are no records, either biblically or by writers of Jewish antiquity, that Jesus had ever been ill himself. (Let us not forget that Jesus was a man (flesh and blood) as are you and I. His sacrifice on the cross would have been meaningless had He not been able to suffer from pain, deprivation of anything as would you or I).

And, after much agony He finally was at the place of execution and they nailed Jesus to the cross and crucified Him with two others who were thieves. Pilate ordered that a sign be placed on the highest point on the cross upon which Christ was nailed. It read, 'Jesus of Nazareth: The King of the Jews!'

Then said the chief priests of the Jews to Pilate, "Write not, The King of the Jews; but that He said, I am King of the Jews."

Pilate responded, saying, "What I have written I have written."

Then the soldiers, when they had crucified Jesus, took His garments, and made four parts, to every soldier a part; and also His coat: now the coat was without seam, woven from the top throughout. They said therefore among themselves, "Let us not rend it, but cast lots for it, whose it shall be." (That the scripture might be fulfilled, 'they parted my raiment among them and for my vesture they cast lots).'

Standing beneath the cross of Jesus was his mother and his mother's sister, Mary, the wife of Cleophas, and Mary Magdalene. When Jesus saw his mother and John standing beside her, he said, "Woman, behold your son!" To John who was one of the twelve disciples, He said, "Behold your mother!" And from that hour on, John took Jesus' mother into his own home to care and provide for her.

After this, Jesus knowing that all things were now accomplished, that the scripture might be fulfilled, said, "I thirst." Now there was set a vessel full of vinegar: and they filled a sponge with vinegar, and put it upon hyssop, and put it to His mouth. When Jesus therefore had received the vinegar, He said, "It is finished: and He bowed his head, and gave up the ghost."

Jesus had died. His mission was completed. He had accomplished, thus far, what He had come to do. He had given His life for the sins of the world. But, was His mission complete? In a sense, it was. But, He still had more to do.

Then came the soldiers, and broke the legs of the first, and of the other which was crucified with Him. But when they came to Jesus, and saw that He was dead already, they broke not His legs: But one of the soldiers with a spear pierced His side, and then came there out blood and water.

These things were done, that the scripture should be fulfilled. "A bone of Him shall not be broken."

And again another scripture said, "They shall look on Him whom they pierced."

After this Joseph of Arimathea, being a disciple of Jesus, but secretly, for fear of the Jews, besought Pilate that he might take away the body of Jesus: and Pilate gave him leave. He came therefore, and took the body of Jesus.

Nicodemus, he who came to Jesus in the night, also came bringing with him about a hundred pound weight of myrrh and aloes.

They took Jesus' body and wound it in linen clothes with the spices as is the manner and custom of the Jews when burying. In the place where He was crucified, there was a garden. And in the garden there was a new sepulcher. There laid they Jesus therefore because of the Jews' preparation day; for the sepulcher was nigh at hand.

*****

Many Christians believe that 1 Peter 3:18-20 is telling of Jesus' activity during the three days He was in the grave.

"For Christ also ^{m}suffered[2] ^{n}once for sins, the righteous for the unrighteous, ^{o}that He might bring us to God, being put to death ^{p}in the flesh but made alive ^{q}in the spirit, 19 in which[3] He went and ^{q}proclaimed[4] to the spirits in prison, 20 because[5] they formerly did not obey, ^{r}when God's patience waited in the days of Noah, ^{s}while the ark was being prepared, in which a few, that is, ^{t}eight persons, were brought safely through water."

*****

In trying to understand or comprehend the above verse of scripture I read where Christ (God) was put to death in the flesh (God-Man) but made alive in the spirit (when crucified His flesh died but His spirit became alive). He went (Jesus went) to proclaim to the spirits in prison (those already in Hades (hell)) and, those; the eight were brought safely through water. Jesus, during the time He spent in the tomb descended into death to proclaim to those already sentenced to everlasting torment that He had died for the sins of the world and the way had been provided for them to cast off their present status and live. In other words, Jesus, during His time in the grave visited hell and proclaimed the "good news".

*****

PUT YOUR TRUST
IN THE LORD!

*****

Chapter XVII

The Stone is rolled away – He is risen!
Jesus Appears to His Disciples
Doubting Thomas
Feed My Sheep

While it was still dark, the first day of the week, Mary Magdalene came to the sepulcher where they had placed the body of Jesus. As soon as she arrived, she saw that the stone had been rolled away from the entrance of the tomb. She turned and ran to find Simon Peter and John and shouted, excitedly, "They had taken away our Lord from the sepulcher and we know not where they have laid Him!"

When the two disciples heard this they dropped what they were doing and quickly hurried to the sepulcher to see for themselves. John, having outrun Peter arrived first and entered the sepulcher and saw the linens that were used to wrap Jesus lying on the floor. When John and Peter saw the empty tomb and the linens and napkin they wrapped Jesus' head in, they were full of belief. Unaware of the prophecy that had foretold the event/happening, they turned and went to their home.

But Mary did not leave with John and Simon Peter. She stood there, crying, for a minute or two. Then, she stooped down and looked into the sepulcher and saw two angels in white, sitting, the one at the head and the other at the feet of where the body of Christ had lain. And they asked Mary, "Why are you weeping?"

"Because they have taken away my Lord and I don't know where they have laid Him," Mary cried. She waited for a reply but received none. So, she turned and saw Jesus standing, but she didn't know He was Jesus.

Jesus spoke to Mary, asking her, "Woman, why do you weep? Who are you looking for?"

Mary, supposing that the man before her was the gardener, replied "Tell me sir where you have laid Him and I will take his body away."

Then, Jesus spoke to Mary softly, saying "Mary."

When Jesus had spoken her name, Mary reacted with a wonderful excitement, saying "Master!"

Immediately, Jesus backed away a step or two and said, "Do not touch me for I have not yet ascended to my Father! Go to my brethren (the disciples) and tell them 'I ascended unto my Father, and your Father; to my God: and your God!'"

Mary, reverently, bowed her head and when she looked up again, Jesus was gone. She quickly stood and hurried to tell the disciples. She told them that she had seen the Lord and the things He had said to her.

Later, that same day, in the evening, where the disciples had met secretly for fear of the Jews, Jesus came and stood among them. "Peace be to all of you," He said. He showed them His hands and His side. Then were the disciples glad, when they had seen the Lord. Then said Jesus to them again, "Peace be unto you: as my Father has sent me, even so send I you."

Then, Jesus breathed on them and said, "Receive the Holy Ghost."

*****

We must pause here for a brief discussion as to when the disciples received the Holy Ghost. Many believe that the Holy Ghost came upon the disciples when Jesus breathed on them and made His declaration saying, "Receive the Holy Ghost!" There is no question that what Jesus had said, was said. Biblical scholars insist that the disciples received the Holy Ghost as described in St. John 20:22

indicating that they were, at the time, "born again." But, most feel they had not, at that time, received the _power_ of the Holy Ghost. That doesn't make sense to me because Jesus added, "Whosesoever sins you remit: they are remitted. And, whosoever sins you retain, they are retained." In this statement, Jesus had given them the power to forgive sin on earth! In light of the fact that only God can forgive sin, the Holy Ghost, being the third part of the Trinity; that is to say, God, also, having come upon the disciples as Jesus declared, makes me to understand that the Holy Ghost came upon the disciples as is indicated in John 20:22.

Now, when we look at Acts 2:1-4 we read, "And when the day of Pentecost was fully come, they were all with one accord in one place. ²And suddenly there came a sound from heaven as of a rushing mighty wind and it filled all the house where they were sitting. ³And there appeared unto them cloven tongues like as of fire and it sat upon each of them. ⁴And they were all filled with the Holy Ghost and began to speak with other tongues, as the Spirit gave them utterance."

I understand these verses of scripture to inform us that since the disciples were _already_ filled with the Holy Ghost as announced in verse four (and they were all filled with the Holy Ghost; or, could have been meant to read; _because_ they were all filled with the Holy Ghost _already_) the event as outlined in Acts Chapter 2 unfolds as described.

We could be arguing semantics because there can be no greater power than the power to forgive one of his or her sins. When Jesus announced to the disciples that they had received the Holy Ghost in St. John 20:22, He was telling them that the power of God was in them. How can I say this? I can say this because I believe that the Holy Ghost is the third Person in the God-Head. Thus, when Jesus breathed on the disciples in St. John 20:22 and declared that they "Receive ye the Holy Ghost"; Jesus wasn't saying that they are to receive some now and some later. Jesus declared it in St. John 20:22 and that was when they received the Holy Ghost. This, of course, meant that as of that moment, the power of God was within them. There can be no argument concerning the above if we believe in the Triune God and, if we believe, that there can be no greater power than the power to forgive sin.

*****

When Jesus was in the room with the disciples at that time, we are informed that the apostle Thomas was not present. When the disciples had told Thomas, later, that they had seen the Lord, Thomas told them, "Except I shall see in His hands the print of the nails, and put my finger into the print of the nails, and thrust my hand into His side, I will not believe."

Eight days later (there is no record of where the resurrected Jesus had been and what He was doing these eight days) when the disciples were in the same room; Thomas being with them, Jesus appeared and stood in their midst and said, "Peace be to all of you. He then turned to face Thomas and said, "Thomas, reach with your finger and behold my hands; and reach with your hand, and thrust it into my side: and be not faithless, but believing."

And Thomas answered and said unto Him, "My Lord and my God."

Then Jesus said to Thomas, "because you have seen me, you are a believer: blessed are they that have not seen, and yet believe."

The Gospel writer, St. John, closes this chapter by

writing, "And many other signs truly did Jesus in the presence of his disciples, which are not written in this book: But these are written, that ye might believe that Jesus is the Christ, the Son of God; and that believing ye might have life through His name." Here he is telling us that there were so many other things Christ had done that he and the other disciples had witnessed and, why he had written, for posterity, and mankind's edification, that which he wrote. *'that ye might believe that Jesus is the Christ, the Son of God; and that believing ye might have life through his name.'*

*****

When Jesus died on the cross and He stated, "It is finished", it was true that what He had come to earth to accomplish was only partially finished. The suffering and the agony He knew beforehand that He was to go through; and the shedding of His blood and death upon the cross was finished; but there was still more to be done. In order for Jesus to really convince His disciples that He was the Son of God, He had to win the victory over death by, putting it simply, come back to life. He had to rise from the grave and "prove" it to them. By appearing to His disciples; that was all the proof they needed.

And, by returning to make sure all the disciples were witness to His "coming back from the grave" (remember, Thomas was not in the room when Jesus first appeared to the disciples) he returned and made sure that not one of them would be able to question His resurrection. After He made sure Thomas was convinced without question, Jesus was speaking to the generations to come when He said, "Blessed are they that have not seen, and yet believe."

*****

The Apostle John further declares that Jesus showed Himself again to the disciples at the sea of Tiberius; There were together Simon Peter, and Thomas called Didymus, and Nathanael of Cana in Galilee, and the sons of Zebedee, and two other of his disciples.

Simon Peter said unto them, I go fishing. They say unto him, "We, also, go with you." They went forth, and entered into a ship immediately; and that night they caught nothing.

But when the morning was now come, Jesus stood on the shore: but the disciples knew not that it was Jesus. Then Jesus said unto them, "Children, have ye any meat?"

They answered him, "No."

And He said unto them, "Cast the net on the right side of the ship, and ye shall find." They cast therefore, and now they were not able to draw it for the multitude of fishes.

Therefore that disciple whom Jesus loved said unto Peter, "It is the Lord!" Now when Simon Peter heard that it was the Lord, he girt his fisher's coat unto him, (for he was naked,) and did cast himself into the sea.

And the other disciples came in a little ship; (for they were not far from land, but as it were two hundred cubits,) dragging the net with fishes. As soon then as they were come to land, they saw a fire of coals there, and fish laid thereon, and bread.

And Jesus cried out to them, saying "Bring of the fish which you have now caught!"

Peter went and pulled the net to shore and counted 153 large fish. All were surprised that the net did not break. Now, the Gospel does not tell who cooked the fish, but we are told that Jesus cried out, "Come! Let us dine!" He broke bread and offered it to His disciples. Not one of the disciples questioned who the man was. They knew, unquestionably, that He was their Lord, Jesus Christ.

*****

Taking license as a writer here; not taking away from the message of the Gospel, I assume that while the disciples were dining with Jesus on the shore, they talked. Surely, they wouldn't just sit on the beach eating with a Man who is the Son of God and not utter a word. There had to be lots of questions some, if not all of Jesus' disciples, wanted to ask. And, assuming questions were asked I'm assuming that Jesus wouldn't just tell them to remain silent and eat.

One of the questions I would ask would have been, "Master, what was going through your mind when you were dying on the cross?" I would ask, "What were you thinking about?" I wonder what Jesus' answer to me might have been.

Putting myself in His place I ask myself the same question. What do I think would have been on my mind as I looked out over the crowd of people watching while I was dying? I'd be looking down at my mother, Mary, and my Apostle John, and, also, many who were there who hated me.

Lots of people insist that when a person is dying, their whole life is revealed to them, in their mind. Jesus was on the cross for a lot of hours before he died. Surely, His mind had to be on something. Was He thinking about His childhood friend Thomas and the wonderful times He had with Mary and His earthly father, Joseph? Was He wondering if it was necessary that He suffer such a humiliating death; death by crucifixion? Could He have been thinking that maybe He could have done something different; anything that could have brought about the same results without the need for Him to have gone through so much suffering and pain?

But, we cannot put ourselves in Jesus' place because He is God and we are not. He thinks as God and we can only think as do men. Perhaps Jesus thought of nothing at all except His Mother, Mary. I believe this because He made sure that the Apostle John knew that he (John) was to take Mary into his home and care for her needs from that moment on. Another thing on Jesus' mind had to be the ordeal he had gone through because when He knew death was coming, He said, "It is finished!"

In the Gospel of St. Luke 23:34 the author has Jesus saying, "Father, forgive them for they know not what they do." By this saying, I am believing that Jesus was conscious of the fact that some of those who called for His crucifixion and had been party to what was taking place, could have had second thoughts about calling for Jesus' death and were sorry for what their actions had brought about. To these people, Jesus, by saying what he did, caused them to "rest easy" because He wanted to let them know they were already forgiven for what they've done.

Many have inferred that Jesus while going through the torment previous to His death might have been thinking of Mary Magdalene, and other earthly matters that a mere man, not a God, would be thinking. This is nonsense and such inference should be disregarded as sacrilegious and hypocritical. Anyone who says he or she believes in God, Jesus Christ, and the Holy Ghost, and feels that Jesus could have had carnal thoughts, or thoughts of lust and worldly matters while suffering and making the ultimate sacrifice for our sins is a fool and not worthy, in my opinion, of the blessings of God.

*****

So when they had dined, Jesus said to Simon Peter,

"Simon, son of Jonas, loves thou me more than these?

Peter replied quickly, "Lord, you know that I love you.

And then Jesus said, "Feed my sheep."

Jesus asked Peter a second time, "Peter, do you love me?"

"Yes, Lord," Peter said. "You know that I love you."

Again, the Lord said, "Feed my sheep."

Jesus asked Peter a third time, "Peter do you love me?"

Peter, of course, was getting grieved because Jesus kept asking him, "Peter, do you love me?" Peter answered quickly, "You know I love you."

"Feed my sheep," Jesus replied. And then Jesus continued, "When you were young you prepared and went where, at times, you didn't really want to go. But," Jesus said, "when you get old you'll stretch out your arms and another will prepare you and lead you to places you may not want to go." After He had spoken these words, He looked into Peter's eyes and said, "Follow me."

As Peter was walking alongside Jesus He turned about and saw that John was following close behind. Peter had more questions to ask Jesus as they were walking. "Lord," he asked, "which of us betrayed you?" He added, "What is to become of he that betrayed you?"

The Lord replied, "If I ask him to tarry until I come; what is that to you? Follow me." What Jesus was telling Peter was that he should mind his own business! I am telling you to follow me and feed my sheep. What is to become of another should not concern you."

Then went this saying abroad among the brethren, that that disciple should not die: yet Jesus said not unto him, He shall not die; but, if I will that he tarry till I come, what is that to thee?

*****

In the scripture above, Jesus is not only talking to Peter; He is, in fact, talking to every priest, minister, and lay person who has any knowledge concerning Him. He is telling those of us who love and understand Christ' message to make sure His sheep are fed.

Christ is the Son of God; the Good Shepherd. His instructions to us are that we assist Him by feeding His sheep; that we assist Him in tending the sheep. We are to feed His sheep with the good news that Christ came to give us life. We are to tell the world that He died for our sins on the cross. We are to feed His sheep with the news that because of His sacrifice, we are reconciled to His Father in heaven. We are to do His work until He returns to separate the sheep from the goats.

By answering His call to feed His sheep, we are obedient to Him and we please Him. If we have the knowledge of what He requires of us and we are not obedient to Him, we displease Him and we ourselves are lost. It is He from whom we receive our talents and gifts to be used in His service. If we do not use the gifts and talents given us, we are useless to Him. In other words, those who follow Jesus and obey righteousness walk with Him in His glory. These are the ones who will receive the gift of God which is everlasting life. These are the children of Christ who sit to the right of the Father.

"Feed my sheep! Tend to the flock!" Jesus says. He, also, makes it clear that we should not be concerned about what others do concerning Him, or what His intentions for others might be. "Feed my sheep!" the Lord instructs. He is telling the world not to be concerned with how He will judge anyone else (the Judas's). We are to do what we are supposed to do and not look back.

The Gospel of St. Matthew Chapter 25:41-46 gives us a

good idea of what could happen to the disobedient. "Then shall he say also unto them on the left hand, Depart from me, ye cursed, into everlasting fire, prepared for the devil and his angels: For I was an hungered, and ye gave me no meat: I was thirsty, and ye gave me no drink: I was a stranger, and ye took me not in: naked, and ye clothed me not: sick, and in prison, and ye visited me not. Then shall they also answer him, saying, Lord, when saw we thee an hungered, or athirst, or a stranger, or naked, or sick, or in prison, and did not minister unto thee? Then shall he answer them, saying, "Verily I say unto you, inasmuch as ye did *it* not to one of the least of these, ye did *it* not to me. And these shall go away into everlasting punishment: but the righteous into life eternal." St. Matthew 25:41-46.

*****

Verse 23 of the final chapter of St. John reads: Then went this saying abroad among the brethren, that that disciple should not die: yet Jesus said not unto him, He shall not die; but, If I will that he tarry till I come, what is that to thee? In this verse of scripture is Jesus telling Peter that John shall not die? He could be saying this concerning John because Jesus could have noticed a bit of envy in Peter's eyes when Peter turned to see John was following he and the Lord.

However, most theologians believe that St. John the Apostle, "the disciple who Jesus loved" died a natural death at the age of 94. It is believed that St. John outlived all the other apostles.

Some legends say that John did not die but ascended like Elijah. St. Augustine notes a tradition that when John was buried, the ground heaved as if the apostle were still breathing.

But, it was not Jesus who said he shall not die. It was the brethren. Why this rumor went about among the brethren no one knows except that; perhaps the Lord loved John so much He didn't want John to experience death.

Yet, there is also the thought that perhaps when Jesus responded to Peter's question as to what is to become of he that betrayed you; it is thought that perhaps the question of death concerned Judas since he was the betrayer. We know Judas hanged himself as is indicated in the scripture. So Judas did die. But, maybe Jesus was telling Peter to mind his own business concerning Judas and the hereafter. Jesus might have been telling Peter that Judas will tarry in the grave as will all others who die until He returns and then He will decide what is to become of "he who betrayed you."

No one really knows who or what Jesus was referring to other than the fact that Jesus was telling Peter to do what he had been called to do. "Feed my sheep! Tend the flock! Don't look back, and don't stick your nose into where it doesn't belong." It doesn't belong where you are in a position of judging anyone.

*****

John, than, states, "I am the Apostle John who is the author of these things which we, my brethren and I, know are true. There are so many other things that I could have told you about concerning Jesus but to have done so would have been impossible. If I were able to write concerning all the wonderful things Jesus said and done, I don't believe that the world would be big enough to contain all the books that would have to be written. Amen (let it be so)."

*****

Pause here to read Psalm 100.
Give God thanks for the many blessings He's given you.

Chapter XVIII

Comments on Same-Sex Marriage
The Bible Is the Inspired Word of God.

"Now I beseech you, brethren, by the name of our Lord Jesus Christ, that _ye all speak the same thing, and that there be no divisions among you_; but that ye be perfectly _joined together in the same mind and in the same judgment._ For _it hath been declared unto me of you_, my brethren... "1 Cor. 1:10-11.

There can be no dispute between those who oppose same sex marriages and those who do not _if both sides agree that the Holy Bible is the inspired Word of God._ A person cannot say he or she believes and accepts one commandment of God but will not accept another. That, of course, makes no sense at all.

Psalm 19 tells us, "The law of the Lord is perfect, converting the soul; the testimony of the Lord is sure, making   wise   the   simple."

Just about every Christian Church agrees that all scripture is written by inspiration from God and that the scriptures constitute the divine rule of Christian faith and practice. If we, as Christians do not accept the Holy Bible as the inspired Word of God, we cannot truly call ourselves Christians.

The Jews do not accept the New Testament because they do not believe what is recorded in the NT books. Therefore, because they do not believe the contents of what is written in the NT; and, because they do not believe that Jesus Christ is the Son of God, they cannot, and do not, call themselves Christians.

We who call ourselves Christians believe the contents of the Old Testament _and_ the New Testament. The Old

Testament tells us of the Creation, the history of the Jewish Nation, and the prophecy of the prophets which, of course, discusses genealogy and all things leading up to the birth of our Savior, Jesus Christ. The New Testament tells us of the birth of our Savior, his teachings, what he requires of us, the miracles he performed, the crucifixion, the resurrection, and his ascension to his Father. Because we affirm our belief concerning Christ, we call ourselves Christians.

Because the scriptures are written by inspiration from God, we accept it as His holy word. Matthew and John, two Apostles of our Lord, walked with Christ; were taught by him; witnessed his miracles, and were on hand when he came to the apostles after the resurrection. Mark knew the apostles and traveled with Paul who talked with the Lord when he was toppled from his mount on route to Damascus. Luke, the physician, also traveled with the Apostle Paul and, early historians of Jewish antiquity inform us that much of what he wrote in his gospel came from Mary, the mother of our Lord and Savior.

2 Tim. 3:16-17 tells us, "[16]All scripture is given by inspiration of God, and is profitable for_doctrine, for reproof, for correction, for instruction in righteousness: [17]That the man of God may be perfect, that is, holy, thoroughly furnished unto all good works."

A person cannot be a "liberal" concerning what God requires of us if we are to call ourselves Christians and attempt to "justify" our relationship with Christ and the Church by trying to put our Lord "on the spot", so to speak. What I mean by that is this; those who attempt to circumvent an issue like homosexuality and lesbianism by saying God is love and the love of a man for a man or a woman for a woman should be just as acceptable as the love of a man for a woman. "God will not be mocked!" Genesis 12:3. Some will tell me that the fact that God will not be mocked in Genesis has nothing at all to do with what I am getting at. The mere fact that those who argue direct statements in the bible cannot win because, in truth; those who try to justify their behavior by telling us God is love and that it doesn't matter if the love is a man in bed with a man or a woman in bed with a woman, is an attempt to mock God by trying to insinuate that there is no difference. There is a difference and the difference is plain and simple and easy to understand.

The Book of Romans clearly speaks of those who disregard the laws of God. Make no mistake that those who turn their backs on the natural order of affection have given themselves to lust, lasciviousness, and fornication and are an *abomination unto the Lord.*

How can anyone who professes to be a Christian argue with the words of the Apostle Paul as indicated in chapter one (1) of the book of Romans? Paul writes the following: "For this cause God gave them up unto vile affections: for even their women did change the natural use into that which is against nature: And likewise also the men, leaving the natural use of the woman, burned in their lust one toward another; men with men working that which is unseemly, and receiving in themselves that recompense of their error which was meet."

Paul continues in Romans, chapter one (1) verses thirty one (31) and thirty-two (32): "Without understanding, covenant breakers, without natural affection, implacable, unmerciful: and, 32: Who knowing the judgment of God, *that they which commit such things are worthy of death*, not only do the same, but have pleasure in them that do them."

The above scripture is clear. *They that commit such*

197

things are worthy of death! **Love is wonderful! It's great for one man to say he loves another man. It's great for one woman to say she loves another woman. But it is not a wonderful thing for them to have sex one with the other!**

If you try to circumvent God's commandments in the name of love; if you try to justify your sinful behavior; disregarding the natural order of nature as created by God; why, then, wouldn't it be alright for one to have sex with one's sister, or brother, since the brother loves the sister and the sister loves the brother? We'd have to forget about what incest is because it would no longer mean anything. If a woman loves her dog or cat; why, then, wouldn't it be appropriate for that woman to have sex with her dog, or cat? We'd have to also forget about "bestiality" because that would no longer apply. I realize I have gone to an extreme in making a point but, there are many who are fanatically attached to their pets. And, in well-knit families, the bonds of love are very strong.

If we as a society of Christians say that, in the name of love, it's quite alright to disregard what the Lord calls an abomination, what then will stop the Church from forgetting about what's in God's word and write its own book of religion?

Many clergymen have already set aside what God says and are supportive of those who fornicate. And, that's exactly what those women who wed women, and those men, who marry men, are doing.

I have knowledge of many influential people and clergymen who have, and still do, preach the word of God but, when learning that one of *their* children were gay, have found their behavior acceptable even though God's word says it is wrong! If the Apostle Paul writes that homosexuality is an abomination, do we say he is wrong?

Perhaps, then, we ought to scour through everything he's written and begin to scratch out other things as well.

When we are ill and are told to take a certain medicine that tastes awful, we take it because it's what the doctor prescribes. It is possible that if we don't do as the doctor orders; or do not have an operation the doctor tells us we must have; we could die. So it is with God; he tells us what we must do to live and how we must behave if we are to please him. If we do as he says we will live again. He tells us this in no uncertain terms. The language is clear and precise. If we obey his commandments, and do as he requires, we will have everlasting life. If we do not; we will die.

We are not God! Our Father in heaven is God! If we believe in him with all our hearts and with all our minds; we accept him and his son, Christ Jesus, and the Holy Ghost. God can do no wrong. We who love him know this and should abide by his word as given to us in the Holy Bible.

The bible is the very foundation of our belief in our heavenly Father. The Holy Bible is our book of instructions that must be followed. 2 Tim. 2:15 tells us "Study to show thyself approved unto God, a workman that needeth not to be ashamed, rightly dividing the Word of Truth."

Those of you who are confused about what God requires us to do; how he expects us to behave, must study the word of God to learn. As you study, you will learn the truth about God and, if you are sincere about being a Christian, you will be obedient to Him. You will live a life of "truth" concerning Him. God is Truth and there is no way that any one of us can be a Christian if we do not worship Him in truth!

Those ministers and others who represent a Church and

199

support same sex marriages have placed their salvation in jeopardy. It's not good enough for them to say, "They love each other so it's alright for them to live together as a married couple." Those who approve of same sex marriages and still believe they are pleasing God are living a lie.

In the Garden of Eden, God said, "It is not good that the man should be alone," so he made woman to be with the man; a companion; someone to satisfy man's needs (Genesis 2:18). God did not make a man for the man. He said that it was not good for the man to be alone so he made a woman for the man! God did this! Do those of you who support same sex marriages believe that God should have made a man to be with the man?

Some of you might tell me that he had to make the woman because how else could there be pro-creation? That argument is ridiculous because the woman was only told she would have to suffer the agony of child birth later; after the woman disobeyed God. Plain and simple; woman was made for the man to satisfy man's needs! The man and the woman were made by God in order to complement each other, physically.

The Lord God made no mistake in creating the woman for the man. In making the woman, God demonstrated his perfection of thought and his extraordinary incomparable genius!

The Gospel of St. Matthew tells us, Jesus said, "Be perfect; even as your Father in heaven is perfect!" God is perfect in everything he does; everything he created; in all that he requires of all of us. He is holy and perfect! And, who are we to say that he is not!

You tell me, "Why did God make a man and woman gay? If the man is only attracted to other men and the woman attracted to other woman; whose fault is that?" You could tell me whatever you want insisting that all the gay people, being born that way, are entitled to happiness and should be able to live with those they love because that's what God is all about!

To begin, as some are born with abnormalities that are physical, research tells us that about 10% of those born are born where their hormones, and the process of the building of female and male hormones, become flawed. Thus a child who is a male develops having more female hormones and the female develops having more male hormones. Thus, the baby, in essence, is born "gay". In a similar way to this but in different amounts of the hormones, bisexuals are born. This is the most likely explanation to this mystery and is being scientifically investigated.

Other investigations lean towards just the opposite conclusion. When a child is born a female, it is because the overwhelming hormones in that child are female hormones and so it is when a child is born a male. As the child grows and develops, if a female, the female hormones control the physicality of the person and so it is with the male.

Nevertheless, in assuming there is a flaw in the hormone processing of a child, and the child consequently leans towards being gay, does this mean that the child must live as a gay person? The mere fact that the person might be gay because of a physical abnormality to do with hormones tells us that being gay is not normal. God made us to be perfect because *he* is perfect. When we say that God made us; what we are saying is that God created man and woman in such a way that they are able to procreate and multiply.

Many things made to be one way, over time, because of many reasons, develop problems until they are no longer in their original state. When God made the man and the woman, perfect, physically, and put them <u>out</u> of the Garden of Eden, life became completely different from how God wanted it to be for his creation.

In the Garden, for example, God's creation had the best food to eat and was not susceptible to disease and sickness and conditions that would, and could, alter an individual's physical viability. They were perfect, living in a perfect environment under the protection of God himself. God, once they were put out of the Garden of Eden, would no longer make any decisions concerning anything that had to do with his creations' health and mental stability. Man would eat what he wanted, do what he wanted, go where he chose; and take chances and risks' he wouldn't have had to take if he was still in the Garden of Eden. Many factors cause imperfection to come from perfection.

There were no germs and viruses in the Garden of Eden and nor were the animals hostile until Adam and Eve were put out of the Garden. *So, that which was made perfect evolved into imperfection because of man's actions and behavior.*

God does not control our lives and allows us to make our own decisions. The decisions we make often determine how successful we become and, in essence, if we are healthy or not. Thus, God has no part in whether a person leans towards being gay or, even, if, as some researchers say, are born gay. Being gay is an abnormality and it is wrong. Even if, through no fault of one's own, a person is gay, adjustments can be made and should be made.

Those who are alcoholics and are addicted to drugs eventually come to the realization that to continue in their ways could cost them their lives. So, they go to clinics and seek those who are trained to help. The use of illegal drugs and drinking alcohol in excess are probably the hardest things to overcome. Some find it impossible to give up the use of tobacco and many, research shows, get cancer because of its use. We know we should not use illegal drugs and drink alcohol excessively; and, it is extremely dangerous to be smoking. The use of these products can cause our death.

And, so it is with fornication and lust. It is unnatural for a man to be intimate, sexually, with another man as it is with women. God tells us that he does not approve of it. He tells us that if we conduct our lives having such behavior we will die.

The Lord God wants all of us to live and he gives us alternatives to fornication, lust, lasciviousness, and this kind of unnatural behavior. Every one of us is able to live without having sex. So there is no excuse for displeasing God by living a "sinful" life. Many have sought help from professionals and are now enjoying life, normally. Homosexuals and lesbians have, with the proper help, been able to put those ways of life behind them and, now, have families and look forward to God's reward when their lives on earth are through.

Others have become priests' and nuns and have dedicated themselves to serving God and helping others in the Church. While it is true that many of these have broken their vows of celibacy they amount to but a few compared to the great number of those who have done this. Still others have given up sex altogether for fear of losing their souls.

*****

It should be clear that I am opposed to same sex marriages because this kind of behavior greatly displeases God. And the word of God tells us explicitly that those who conduct their lives in such a way will die! The word of God does not tell us that these people *might* die, or *could* die. The word of God makes it very clear that these people *will* die!

I fail to understand why Christians even debate this issue. Jesus Christ tells us in St. Matthew chapter 19 that marriage is between a man and a woman. Jesus said in verse 4, "Have ye not read that he which made them at the beginning made them male and female?" What could be clearer than this?

But, the Apostle Paul discusses marriage. According to him, marriage hinders the work of the Lord. As far as he was concerned; and I agree with him; those who truly love the Lord should not find it difficult not marrying. Read 1 Cor. 7 and learn what he says about marriage.

I will not continue to belabor the point I know I have made. My views concerning my attitude on same sex marriage is that; to God, it is an abomination and punishable by death (that is to say; it is a sin and "the soul that sinneth, it shall die (Ezekiel 18:20)."

I have said previously that there can be no dispute between those who oppose same sex marriages and those that do not *if both sides agree that the Holy Bible is the inspired Word of God.* If you accept the Holy Bible as the foundation of our religion, than to support same sex marriage is sinful and death is imminent; not just to those who practice it but to those who condone it, as well. There is no doubt that too many that choose to circumvent what the Holy Bible teaches, their religion and faith in Jesus Christ, is to worship and do so at their convenience. It can prove difficult, at times, to live a true Christian life but, we must all know that one must make sacrifices and stand fast.

I could go on and on with proof from the Holy Bible that

same sex marriage is sinful and its practice an abomination. I know that what I have said, above, cannot be disputed. I am a person who loves all people and continuously prays that those who do not agree with me, or who just don't want to accept what the word of God teaches, because they are weak or who give in to unnatural desires of the flesh; I urge them to seek God in prayer through Christ Jesus for strength and forgiveness so that they too, like the Apostle Paul can say, ""I have fought a good fight, I have finished my course, I have kept the faith. Henceforth there is laid up for me a crown of righteousness ..." (2 Thes. 4:7, 8) May God bless all of you.

*****

The Parables and Miracles of Jesus

The parables told by Jesus, as mentioned, are not mentioned in the Gospel of St. John but can be found in the Canonical Gospels (synoptic) and in some of the non-canonical Gospels. Parables were a key part of Jesus' teachings. Because they are the words of Jesus Christ, Christians place high emphasis on these parables. According to the Gospel of St. John they are believed to be what the *Father* taught (John 8:28 and 14:10).

The parables of Jesus seem simple and the stories are memorable. However, many scholars have commented that, though they seem simple, the messages they convey are deep. Many of Jesus' parables refer to simple everyday things, such as a woman baking bread (<u>parable of the Leaven</u>), a man knocking on his neighbor's door at night (<u>parable of the Friend at Night</u>), or the aftermath of a roadside mugging (<u>parable of the Good Samaritan</u>). But, on the whole, the parables have major religious themes such as the growth of the <u>Kingdom of God</u>, the importance of prayer, and the meaning of <u>love</u>. In essence, the parables of Jesus Christ are some of the best known stories in the world.

The word parable can also refer to a riddle. In all times in their history the Jews were familiar with teaching by means of <u>parables</u> and a number of parables also exist in the <u>Old Testament</u>. The use of parables by Jesus was hence a natural teaching method that fit into the tradition of His time. The parables of Jesus have been quoted, taught, and discussed since the very beginnings of <u>Christianity</u>.
http://en.wikipedia.org/wiki/Parables_of_Jesus

The synoptic Gospels, Matthew, Mark, and Luke, contain the parables of Jesus. The Gospel of St. John contain only the stories of the "vine" and "good shepherd" which some consider to be parables. Many of the well know spiritual authors have commented that "parables are noticeably absent from the Gospel of John".

Jesus' disciples asked him, "Why do you speak to the people in parables? (St. Matthew 13:10)" And Jesus replied, "Because it has been given to you to know the mysteries of the kingdom of heaven, but to them it has not been given. For whoever has, to him more will be given, and he will have abundance; but whoever does not have, even what he has will be taken away from him. Therefore I speak to them in parables, because seeing they do not see, and hearing they do not hear, nor do they understand. And in them the prophecy of Isaiah is fulfilled, which says:
'Hearing you will hear and shall not understand, and seeing you will see and not perceive; for the hearts of this people have grown dull. Their ears are hard of hearing,

and   their   eyes   they   have   closed,

Lest they should see with their eyes and hear with their ears,

Lest they should understand with their hearts and turn, So that I should¹ heal them.'"

The purpose of the parables Jesus spoke, primarily, was to edify/instruct/teach those who came to hear Him. As mentioned; it is clear that the Father wanted Jesus to teach using parables; the parables being categorized involving different, specific themes. For example: *The following parables have to do with the Kingdom of Heaven: hearing, seeking, and growing.*

1   The Parable of the Sower
2   The Parable of the Hidden Treasure
3   The Parable of the Pearl
4   The Parable of the Growing Seed
5   The Parable of the Mustard Seed
6   The Parable of the Leaven

The following are Parables of loss and redemption:
6   The Parable of the Lost Sheep
7   The Parable of the Lost Coin
8   The Parable of the Prodigal Son

The following are Parables of love and forgiveness:
9   The Parable of the Two Debtors
10 The Parable of the Unforgiving Servant
11 The Parable of the Good Samaritan

The following are Parables about prayer:

12 **The Parable of the Friend at Night**

13 **The Parable of the Unjust Judge**

14 **The Parable of the Pharisee and the Publican**

*****

The following are Parables to do with Eschatology (those things that have to with final events. The end of the world; Christ's return; the Rapture, etc.).

15 **The Parable of the Faithful Servant**

16 **The Parable of the Ten Virgins**

17 **The Parable of the Grand Banquet**

18 **The Parable of the Rich Fool**

19 **The Parable of the Wicked Husbandmen**

20 **The Parable of the Tares**

21 **The Parable of the Net**

22 **The Parable of the Budding Fig Tree**

23 **The Parable of the Barren Fig Tree**

The following are other Parables of Jesus:

24 **The Parable of the Wise and Foolish Builders**

25 **The Parable of the Lamp Under a Bushel**

26 **The Parable of the Unjust Steward**

27 **The Parable of the Rich Man and Lazarus**

28 **The Parable of the Talents**

29 **The Parable of the Workers in the Vineyard**

*****

For those of you who are not familiar with where to find the above mentioned parables, I have enclosed the following information should you wish to find them in your

Holy Bible.

A sample Gospel harmony for the parables based on the list of key episodes in the Canonical Gospels is presented on the pages below. For the sake of consistency, the information is automatically sub-selected from the main harmony pages in the Gospel harmony article, based on the list of key episodes in the Canonical Gospels. Usually, no parables are associated with the Gospel of John, just allegories. (See below to know where you can find a specific parable in the Bible).

*****

You can find the Parable of The Growing Seed in Mark 4:26-29.

You can find the Parable of The Two Debtors in Luke 7:41-43

Find the Parable of The Lamp under a Bushel in Matt.5:14-15, Mark 4:21-25, and Luke 8:16-18.

Find the Parable of The Good Samaritan in Luke 10:30-37.

Find the Parable of the Friend at Night in Luke 11:5-8.

Find the Parable of The Rich Fool in Luke 12:16-21.

Find the Parable of The Wise and the Foolish Builders in Matthew 7:24-27 and Luke 6:46-49.

Find the Parable of New Wine into Old Wineskins in Matthew 9:17- Mark 2:21-22, and Luke 5:37-39.

Find the Parable of The Strong Man in Matthew 12:29, Mark 3:27, and Luke 11:21-22.

Find The Parable of The Sower in Matthew 13:3-9, Mark 4: 3-9, and Luke 8:5-8

Find the Parable of The Tares in Matthew 13:24-30.

Find the Parable of the Growing Seed in Mark 4:26-34

Find the Parable of the Barren Fig Tree in Luke 13:6-9.

Find the Parable of the Mustard Seed in Matthew 13:31-32,

Mark 4:30-32, and Luke 13:18-19.

You can find the Parable of <u>The Leaven</u> in Matthew 13, and in Luke 13:20-21.

You can find the Parable of The <u>Hidden Treasure</u> in Matthew 13:44,

Find the Parable <u>Drawing in the Net</u> in Matthew 13:47-50.

Find the Parable <u>Counting the Cost</u> in Luke 14:28-33.

Find the Parable of <u>The Lost Sheep</u> in Matthew 18:10-14 and in Luke 15:4-6.

The Parable of <u>The Unforgiving Servant</u> can be found in Matthew 18:23-35.

The Parable of <u>The Lost Coin</u> can be found in Luke 15:8-9.

You can find the Parable of <u>The Prodigal Son</u> in Luke 15:11-32.

The Parable of <u>The Unjust Steward</u> can be found in Luke 16:1-13.

Find the Parable of the <u>Rich Man and Lazarus</u> in Luke 16:19-31.

<u>The Master and Servant</u> Parable can be found in Luke 17:7-10.

Find the Parable of <u>The Unjust Judge</u> in Luke 18:1-9.

Find the Parable of <u>The Pharisees and the Publican</u> in Luke 18:10-14.

The Parable of <u>The Workers in the Vineyard</u> can be found in Matthew 20:1-16.

The Parable of <u>The Two Sons</u> can be found in Matthew 21:28-32.

Find the Parable of <u>The Wicked Husbandman</u> in Matthew 21:33-41, Mark 12:1-9, and in Luke 20:9-16

Find the Parable of <u>The Great Banquet</u> in Matthew 22:1-14, and in Luke 14:15-24.

The Parable of <u>The Budding Fig Tree</u> can be found in

Matthew 24:32-35, Mark 13:28-31, and in Luke 21:29-33.
The Parable of The Faithful Servant can be found in Matthew 24:42-51, Mark 13:34-37, and in Luke 12:35-48.
Find the Parable of The Ten Virgins in Matthew 25:1-13.
Find the Parable of The Talents or Minas in Matthew 25:14-30, and in Luke 19:12-27.
Find The Sheep and the Goats in Matthew 25:31-46
The Parable of The Wedding Feast can be found in Parallels outside the canonical gospels:

A number of parables have parallels in non-canonical gospels, the Didache, and the letters of Apostolic Fathers. However, given that the non-canonical gospels generally have no time sequence, each Parable as listed is not a Gospel harmony.

*****

The above information concerning the Parables of Jesus is included because no book about Jesus would be complete had it not been included. You now have enough information so that you know why Jesus taught using parables, why they were effective as a teaching tool, and what Jesus accomplished by using the Parable method of edification. And, you now know where to look to find a specific Parable.

*****

Besides familiarizing ourselves with the Parables of Jesus, it is also important that we mention the *miracles of Jesus*. According to the Gospel of St. John, only some of the wonderful things Jesus did and said were recorded. John wrote that "Jesus did many other things as well. If every one of them were written down, even the whole world would not have room for the books that would be written (St. John 21:25)."

In John, Jesus is said to have performed seven

211

miraculous signs that punctuate His ministry, from changing water into wine at the start of His ministry to raising Lazarus from the dead at the end. There are two categories of miracles that Jesus performed; those that affected people and those that had to do with nature. There are three types of healings where an ailment is "cured", exorcisms where demons are cast out, and the resurrection of the dead. One miracle is unique, as is the transfiguration of Jesus in that the miracle happened to Jesus himself.

In the Gospel of St. <u>Matthew 10:8</u> He advised His disciples to heal the sick without payment and stated: "freely ye received, freely give." Jesus told His disciples to heal the sick without payment because, in those days, the high priests, and others (prophets) charged a fee to heal.

Most Christians believe that the miracles of Jesus were actual historical events and that the miracles He performed were an important part of His life. I believe that Jesus performed miracles as evidence of His divinity. The Son of God, Jesus, did experience pain, hunger, and death which were evidences of His being a man, and miracles which was evidence of His divinity. But, make no mistake; Jesus healed the sick, not only to demonstrate His divinity; He healed them, also, because He had compassion and mercy on a sinful and suffering humanity.

In the Gospel of St. John 10:37-38 Jesus says, "Do not believe me unless I do what my Father does. But if I do it, even though you do not believe me, believe the *miracles*; that you may know and understand that the Father is in me, and I in the Father."

Jesus tells all of us that we should believe His miracles so you should know and understand that His Father (God) is in Him and he is in His Father (God). What Jesus was saying was; you should know and understand that what I do comes from the Father. So, if you believe in the Father (God), you should believe the miracles. By Jesus saying the Father is in Him and He is in his Father; He was giving all the credit and glory to God. And, because they, believing in God and knowing that He is omnipotent and all knowing, have no reason to _not_ believe that the miracles Jesus did came from God.

If a man of God prays for the healing of another, he must be sure to inform those who watch and hear that it is the power of the Holy Spirit working through him that cures the individual. Those who witness the event will either believe or not believe that the miracle can only occur if God is in you and you are in the Father. In other words; you must demonstrate your holiness.

Many theologians and church scholars find it difficult to believe biblical accounts of the healings of Christ because there can be no way to prove that they did occur. This, to me, is nonsense because if we believe the Father is the creator and that he is omnipotent, omnipresent, and omniscient, how can we logically doubt the events recorded in the Holy Bible? Theologians should not profess that they love God and Christ, advocating their belief in a Triune God if they need proof that God, who is the Creator, can walk on water, cure the sick, and raise the dead! If we believe in God, we should believe in him completely. No one should carry the banner of Christ unless he or she is wearing the full armor of faith. Paul's letter to the Ephesians 6: 11 tell us to "Put on the whole armor of God; that ye may be able to stand against the wiles of the devil."

"In everything give praise: for this is the purpose of God in Christ Jesus for you." – 1 Thessalonians 5:18. The purpose of Christ is God's revelation for all the world to see, hear, know, and understand. The miracles of Christ are God's revelation to all of us for they confirm Jesus' divinity and His love and mercy to a sinful and suffering society. Have faith in Jesus and the Holy Spirit will make a miracle occur in your life as demonstrated by Christ in the Holy Scriptures.

Jesus, the Son of God, taught the world using parables as His primary tool/method of teaching. In everything He taught, He always affirmed that He was following instructions from His Father in heaven. And, when He healed the leper, opened blind eyes, unstopped deaf ears, cast out demons, and raised the dead, He always said that it was possible because of His Father. In the Gospel of St. John 11 Jesus thanks His Father for hearing His request to bring His friend Lazarus back to life. The scripture reads, "Then they took away the stone from the place where the dead were laid. And Jesus lifted up his eyes and said, 'Father, I thank thee that thou has heard me. And I know that you hear me always: but because of the people which are standing by, I said it, that they may believe that you sent me'" Jesus always gave the glory to His Father. In this case, He, as the event was unfolding, even wanted those who were witnesses to hear Him thanking His Father (God) in heaven so there could be no doubt that it was the Father who made the miracle possible. Nevertheless, in the eyes of all who were there, it was Jesus, the Son of God, who raised Lazarus from the grave.

Jesus, as we all are aware, sits at the right hand of God. God has given Christ great glory in that there is no person who is able to approach Him without going, first, through Christ. In the Gospel of St. John, Jesus makes it clear to all the ages, saying, "I am the way, the truth, and the life: no man cometh unto the Father, but by me." Jesus here was telling Thomas, his apostle, that the only way to where he

214

was going, heaven, was to go through Him.

This book would not have been complete had I not given ample space to the miracles of Jesus Christ. Without going into detail concerning each one of the miracles performed by Jesus, I have included, in this book, the following chart which will tell you where in the Holy Bible you should look if you want to know more.

*****

It should be noted that the <u>Gospel of John</u> specifically states that the miracles it recorded were but a portion of the miracles that Jesus actually performed.

<u>List of Miracles of our Lord Jesus Christ</u>

1. Marriage at Cana: John 2:1-11
2. Exorcism at the Synagogue at Capernaum: Mark 1:21-28, Luke 4:31-37
3. Miraculous draught of fishes: Luke 5:1-11
4. Young man from Nain: Luke 7:11-17
5. Cleansing a leper: Matt. 8:1-4, Mark 1:40-45, Luke 5:12-16
6. The Centurion's servant: Matt. 8:5-13, Luke 7:1-10, John 4:46-54
7. Healing the mother of Peter's wife: Matt. 8:14-17, Mark 1:29-34, Luke 4:38-41
8. Exorcising at sunset: Matt. 8:16-17, Mark 1:32-34, Luke 4:40-41
9. Calming the storm: Matt. 8:23-27 Mark 4:35-41, Luke 8:22-25
10. Gerasenes demonic: Matt. 28:34, Mark 5:1-20, Luke 8:22-25
11. Paralytic at Capernaum: Matt.9:1-8, Mark 2:1-12, Luke 5:17-26
12. Daughter of Jairus raised: Matt. 9:18-26, Mark

5:21-43, Luke 8:50-56

13. The woman with the issue of blood: Matt. 9:20-22, Mark 5:24-34, Luke 8:43-48
14. Two blind men in Galilee: Matt. 9:27-31
15. Exorcising a mute: Matt. 9:32-34
16. Paralytic at Bethesda: John 5:1-18
17. Man with withered hand: Matt. 12:9-13, Mark 3:1-6, Luke 6:6-11
18. Exorcising a blind man and mute man: Matt. 12:22-28, Mark 3:20-30, Luke 11:14-23
19. An infirm woman: Luke 13:10-17
20. Feeding the 5000: Matt. 14:13-21, Mark 6:31-34,, Luke 9:10-17, John 6:5-15
21. Walking on water: Matt. 14:22-33, Mark 6:45-52, John 6:16-21
22. Healing in Gennesaret: Matt, 14:34-36, Mark 6:53-56
23. Canaanite woman's daughter: Matt. 15:21-28 Mark 7:24-30
24. Deaf mute at Decopolis: Mark 7:31-37
25. Feeding of the 4000: Matt. 15:32-39, Mark 8:1-9
26. The blind man of Bethsaida: Mark 8:22-26
27. The Transfiguration of Jesus: Matt. 17:1-13, Mark 9:2-13 Luke 9:28-36
28. The boy demon possessed: Matt. 17:14-21, Mark 9:14-29, Luke 9:37-49
29. A coin in the fish's mouth: Matt. 17:24-27
30. The man with dropsy: Luke 14:1-6
31. Cleansing 10 lepers: Luke 17:11-19
32. Born blind at birth: John 9:1-
33. Blind... near Jericho: Matt. 20:29-34, Mark 10:46- , The raising of Lazarus: John 11:1-44
34. Cursing the fig tree: Matt. 21:18-22, Mark 11:12-14

35. Healing a servant's ear: Luke 22:49-51
36. A catch of 153 fish: John 21:1-24

A list of miracles found other than in the New Testament performed by Jesus are recorded in 2nd Century texts called the Infancy Gospels narrate Jesus performing miracles during His childhood. I have listed them below:

1. A rich man is raised from the dead: Found in the Secret Gospel of Mark 1
2. Water controlled and purified: Found in Infancy Thomas 2.2
3. Birds are made of clay and brought to life: Infancy Thomas 2.3
4. Resurrection of dead playmate Zeno: Infancy Thomas 9
5. He heals a woodcutter's foot: Infancy Thomas 10
6. Held water in His cloak: Infancy Thomas 11
7. Harvested 100 bushels of wheat from 1 seed: Infancy Thomas 12
8. Stretches a board that was too short: Infancy Thomas 13
9. Resurrects a teacher: Infancy Thomas
10. He heals James' viper bite: Infancy Thomas 15
11. He resurrects a dead child: Infancy Thomas 17
12. He resurrects a dead man: Infancy Thomas 18
13. A miraculous virgin birth verified by a midwife: Found in Infancy Thomas 19-20

Some of the information above; and some other information had been supplied by Wikipedia, the free encyclopedia. To learn more about the Miracles of Jesus Christ, visit: Wikipedia on line.

Finally:

It is astonishing to me that those who call themselves Christians keep asking me, "Who was Jesus?" To ask such a question is the indication that he who is asking the question assumes that Jesus _was_ but _is not now!_ If someone were to ask me who Will Rogers was, the question would be appropriate because Will Rogers is dead. But, when I am asked who Jesus was, it is not appropriate simply because Jesus still lives! And, every Christian should know that Christ is alive today as He was 2000 years ago.   We believe Jesus lives because we believe in the resurrection. Had He not risen from the grave, all our hopes and prayers for our restoration and reconciliation with our Father would be meaningless. Christ is alive! Read what Paul writes in 1 Corinthians 15. "Moreover, brethren, I declare unto you the gospel which I preached unto you, which also ye have received, and wherein ye stand; By which also ye are saved, if ye keep in memory what I preached unto you, unless ye have believed in vain.

"For I delivered unto you first of all that which I also received, how that Christ died for our sins according to the scriptures; And that he was buried, and that he rose again the third day according to the scriptures: And that he was seen of Cephas, then of the twelve: After that, he was seen of above five hundred brethren at once; of whom the greater part remain unto this present, but some are fallen asleep. After that, he was seen of James; and then of all the apostles. And last of all he was seen of me."

So, the question should never be, "Who was Jesus." The question should be, "Who is Jesus?" Remember what the word of God tells us, "Jesus Christ the same yesterday, and today, and forever ..." Christ is unchangeable. He is the same today as He was when He walked the earth 2000 years ago. And, because He is the same, He is alive, now. We, as Christians should never dispute this or wonder, or doubt, as did Thomas.

In response to the question, "Who is Jesus?" the answer is simple. He is the Son of God! He is our most trusted and loyal friend! He is not just a passing friend, but one who is always nearby and ready to help us just as long as we love Him as He loves us, and truly believe and accept Him as our deliverer from sin. He redeemed us by His suffering, anguish, and death on the cross. This He did willingly because of His tremendous love for all humanity. Jesus, himself said, "[13]Greater love hath no man than this, that a man lay down his life for his friends (St. John 15:13)." Jesus was not just talk! We have life only because of His death on the cross and His resurrection.

Jesus is the second person in the God-Head. He is the Father's only begotten son. It is through Jesus that we have forgiveness of sin, and because of His resurrection that we have life everlasting, if we live a life that pleases Him.

Above all, we who are Christians must never let our faith waver. It is because of our trust in God and our faith in Jesus Christ that we enjoy the blessings we receive from Him. We must wear the armor of faith continuously so that we can receive that which we expect from Christ; all that He promises the faithful.

All that we do must be done diligently, compassionately, with mercy, and compassion. We must always forgive if we expect forgiveness. When we pray, we should not forget the sick. We must pray for those who are against us; those who do not believe. We must not be ashamed to tell our neighbors, friends, and those we come in contact with that Christ will return to judge us all. Admonish those who ridicule and mock; those who hate and those who are greedy and continue to do what is contrary to Christ's teachings. **If you do all these things you will please God and be saved. Remember what the Scripture says: "⁹Nevertheless, if thou warn the wicked of his way to turn from it; if he does not turn from his way, he shall die in his iniquity; but thou hast delivered thy soul (Ezekiel 33:9)." Amen**

*****

READ THE FOLLOWING VERSE OF SCRIPTURE!
Book of Ezekiel 33:9

*****

I used the Gospel of St. John primarily because it is an account of the public ministry of Jesus Christ. John, supposedly the author of the gospel, describes Jesus as the incarnation of the divine word through whom all things were made. Only in the Gospel of John does Jesus talk at length about himself and His divine role, often shared with His disciples only. John focuses largely on different miracles (including resurrecting Lazarus), given as signs meant to engender faith. Synoptic elements such as parables and exorcisms are not found in John. It presents a realized eschatology in which salvation is already present for the believer. According to the majority viewpoint, the Synoptic, (Matthew, Mark, and Luke), are more historically reliable than John.

I focused mostly on this gospel because the author zeroed in on Jesus in the spiritual sense and not in the physical sense. The author, in my estimation, has already conceded that those who know and believe in Jesus as the Son of God know the miracles He performed and the teachings He preached with the use of parables.

The purpose of this book is to present the spiritual essence of the man, Christ Jesus. Jesus, as mentioned above, speaks at length about Himself in this gospel so there can be no doubt His disciples understood Him since, as John states; most of what Jesus speaks of, at length, in this gospel was meant only for His disciples at the time.

With John's Gospel, the meaning of what Jesus is all about comes shining through. For example, He exemplifies humanity by emphasizing to the disciples that we must be humble. We must practice humility. "The master is not greater than the servant," He taught us. He demonstrated it by the washing of the feet of his disciples. "If I wash your feet," He said, "ought not you to wash each other's feet?" (Paraphrase)

Jesus, God incarnate, wept in the Garden of Gethsemane. He made it clear to Mary and Martha, and the world that <u>He</u> was life and that if you believe, even though you were dead; you will live again.

The greatest example of the power of God that Jesus could demonstrate to His disciples, and to the world, was His power/victory over death. The resurrection of Lazarus made it clear to those who were the witnesses that Christ is God. It was the straw that broke the camels' back as far as the Sadducees and chief priests were concerned and their decision that Jesus had to die.

The author of this gospel also makes it a point to tell the world that Jesus met with the disciples, and others, after the crucifixion in order to add that little something extra to convince those who could otherwise not accept Christ as the Son of God. Even when Thomas expressed doubt when the other disciples had met with Jesus after the resurrection when Thomas was not present; the following meeting when Thomas *was* present and *did* see Jesus, he did believe, completely, the author tells us. And John tells us of the appropriate message Jesus gave to Thomas which was also meant for all generations; "Blessed are those who have not seen and still believe." (Paraphrase)

The message Christ leaves with Peter and the world is that those who know Him should "feed my sheep." Three times he insisted to Peter that he was to go into the world and teach others what He had taught him. This gospel is unlike the synoptic gospels because the emphasis is on the fact that we *know* Christ is the Savior and it is our duty to

tell others about Him; His love and the salvation He offers
to those who believe and accept Him as the Son of God.

*****

*There is a song I use to enjoy singing as a Salvationist
(a soldier in the Salvation Army) many years ago. It's titled,
"I love to tell the Story".* It's a beautiful song and the words
and music have always meant so much to me because they
express how I feel and what's in my heart. If I never write
another book, I will always be content that God inspired
me to write this one. I pray that you will enjoy it and make
it a part of your own home library. I know that as you read
it, God will bless you as He has blessed me.

(Song)
I Love to Tell the Story
Text: Katherine Hankey, 1834-1911
Music: William G. Fischer, 1835-1912
Tune: HANKEY, Meter: 76.76 D with Refrain

1.   I love to tell the story
        Of unseen things above,
        Of Jesus and his glory,
        Of Jesus and his love.
        I love to tell the story,
        because I know 'tis true;
        It satisfies my longings
        as nothing else can do.

Refrain: I love to tell the story,
        'twill be my theme in glory,
        to tell the old, old story

of Jesus and his love.

2.

I love to tell the story;

More wonderful it seems
than all the golden fancies
Of all our golden dreams.
I love to tell the story,
it did so much for me;
and that is just the reason
I tell it now to thee.
(Refrain)

*****

You can go to the following website on the internet and learn the entire song. The site also provides the music so that you can sing it and enjoy the beauty of its message as the songwriters intended. No doubt, you can even order the lyrics and music if you'd like. The site to visit is:
http://www.hymnsite.com/lyrics/umh156.sht

*****

Charles J. Guerra, UCA
Concerning:
Catherine R. Guerra

Catherine, my wife for 45 years was recently called to glory Jan. 4th of 2016. I love her more than anything else in the whole world and miss her very much.

Catherine, while on Earth, served the Lord for many years as a teacher of catechism. She was a loving and caring, conscientious, teacher of the Gospel of Jesus Christ. She taught the children about God's tremendous love for the whole world. She taught them of Christ; why, and how he suffered on the cross that all might be heirs of God's most precious gift of everlasting life. She taught scores of children the Holy Bible, the Church, about the saints, and that it is so important that we love our neighbors, and do works that please God.

Catherine (Kaye) suffered a great deal and it was only because of her deteriorating health that she was forced to give up her work with the Church. Even while she was suffering with cancer and other illnesses (illnesses she kept secret from others) she carried on, loving and serving the Lord for as long as she was physically able. She truly loves the Lord and sacrificed a great deal for the Catholic Church.

My only consolation is in knowing I will be with her again when the Lord calls me home. Not a day passed by that she didn't speak of God's love to me. I will treasure the memories I have of her and look forward to when I can be with her in Christs' heavenly Kingdom. I will always thank God for Catherine (Kaye) my loving, caring wife.

Zachary Cogon
Writes About The Author

Mr. Guerra resides in Pine Bush, New York. I am his son and he has a grandson, John. He has written many books and he has composed many songs. This book, The Prince of Peace, was completed only recently, after his beloved wife Catherine (Kaye) was summoned by God to take her place in His heavenly kingdom.

He studied many years and was ordained an Orthodox Catholic Priest. Prior to becoming a priest he studied privately with several distinguished composers. And even before he had studied and was ordained a presbyter, he studied at Orange County Community College for certification as a Casualty Broker and was later licensed by the State of New York to sell many kinds of insurance.

Now that his loving wife, my mother, is with Christ in Heaven, Mr. Guerra, my dad, is planning a move to Middletown, NY. He plans on living there until God calls him home to be with my mom. You can email my father at cguerra@hvc.rr.com

*****

Other Books Written By Charles J. Guerra:

The Melbourne Street Case
The Mouse, the Owl, and the Fox
The Snalfrocky's: D'Goro Battles the Pindorians
The Chimney Sweeper
Happy Hoppy Hopalong
Barack H. Obama: Ulterior Motives
Candy Kane: Santa's Special Elf
Somebody's killing the Jews
They Murdered My Wife
Sugar Sweet
The Prince of Peace
The Tales of Jonathan Wesley
Until the Judgment
And many others

Please contact us via our Email and we'll send you a brochure you can select from. And be sure to send your prayer requests. Send either by Email or write us at:

Rev. Guerra's website is now under construction and will be ready on or about June 10, 2016.
www.theprinceofpeace.us
Thank you.

Charles J. Guerra
998 Roosa Gap Road
Pine Bush, NY – 12566

www.ingramcontent.com/pod-product-compliance
Lightning Source LLC
Chambersburg PA
CBHW060235050426
42448CB00009B/1455